ESSENCE

DAMIAN
DRACO

ESSENCE

#4

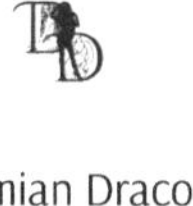

Damian Draco

CONTENTS

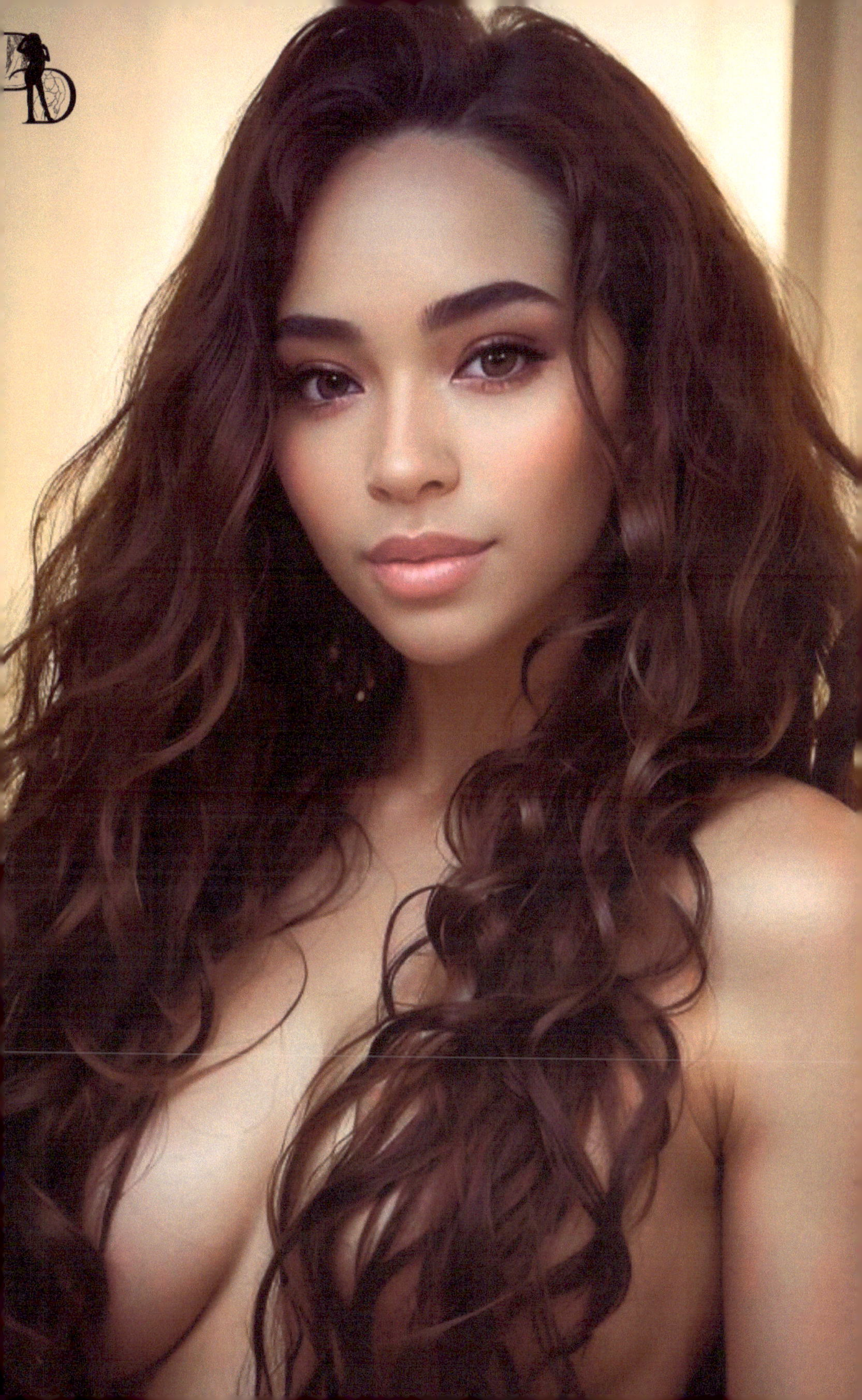

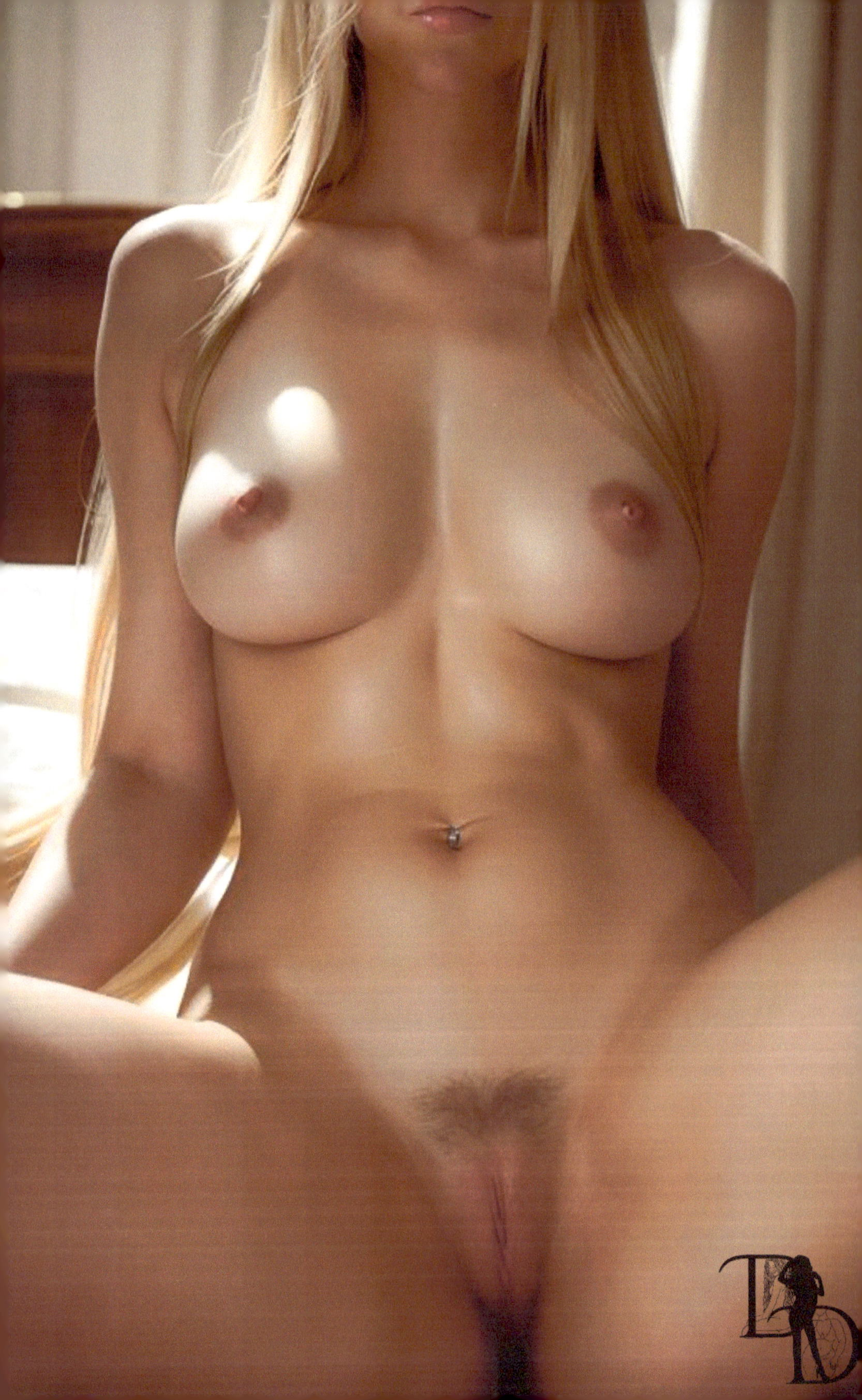

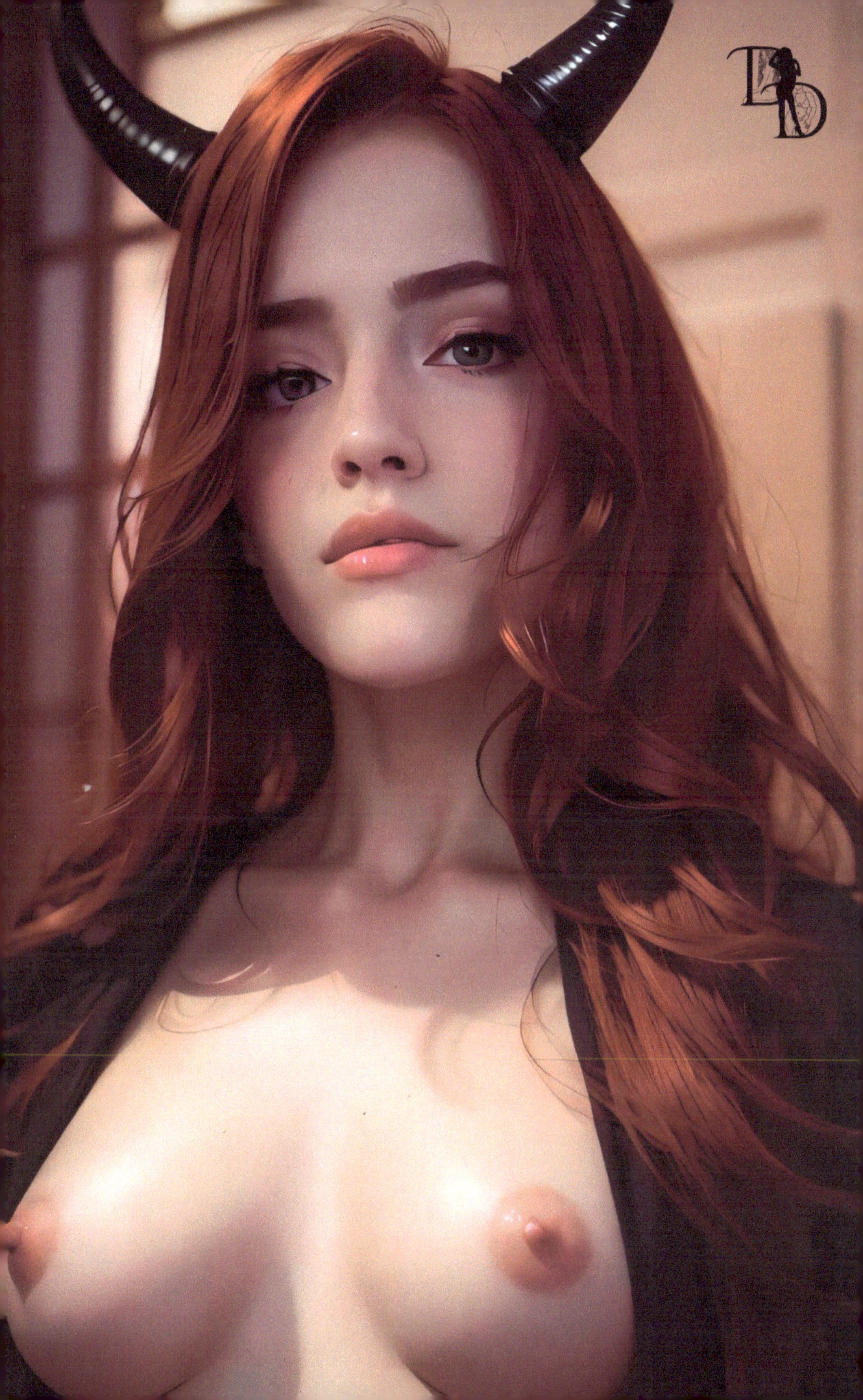

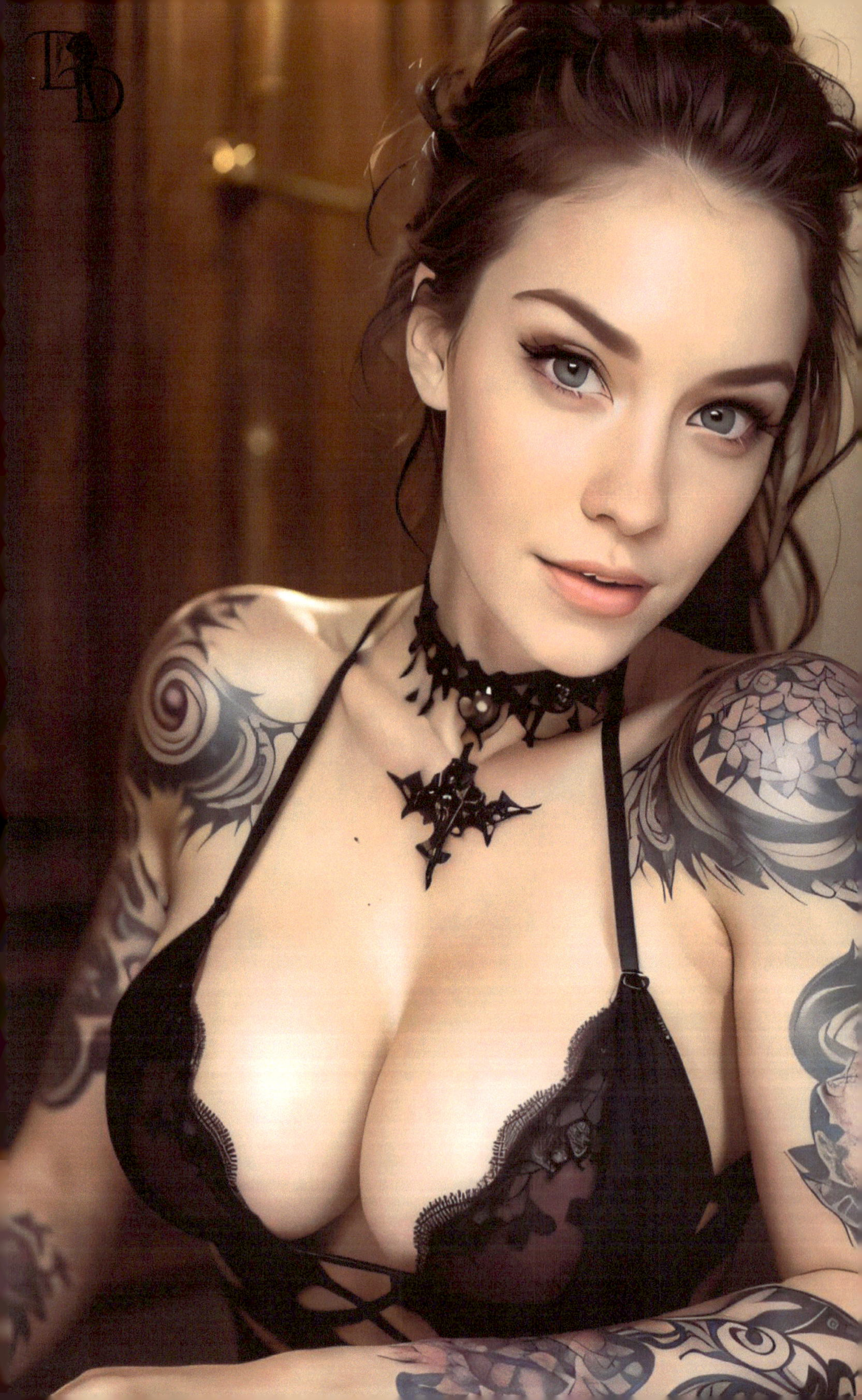

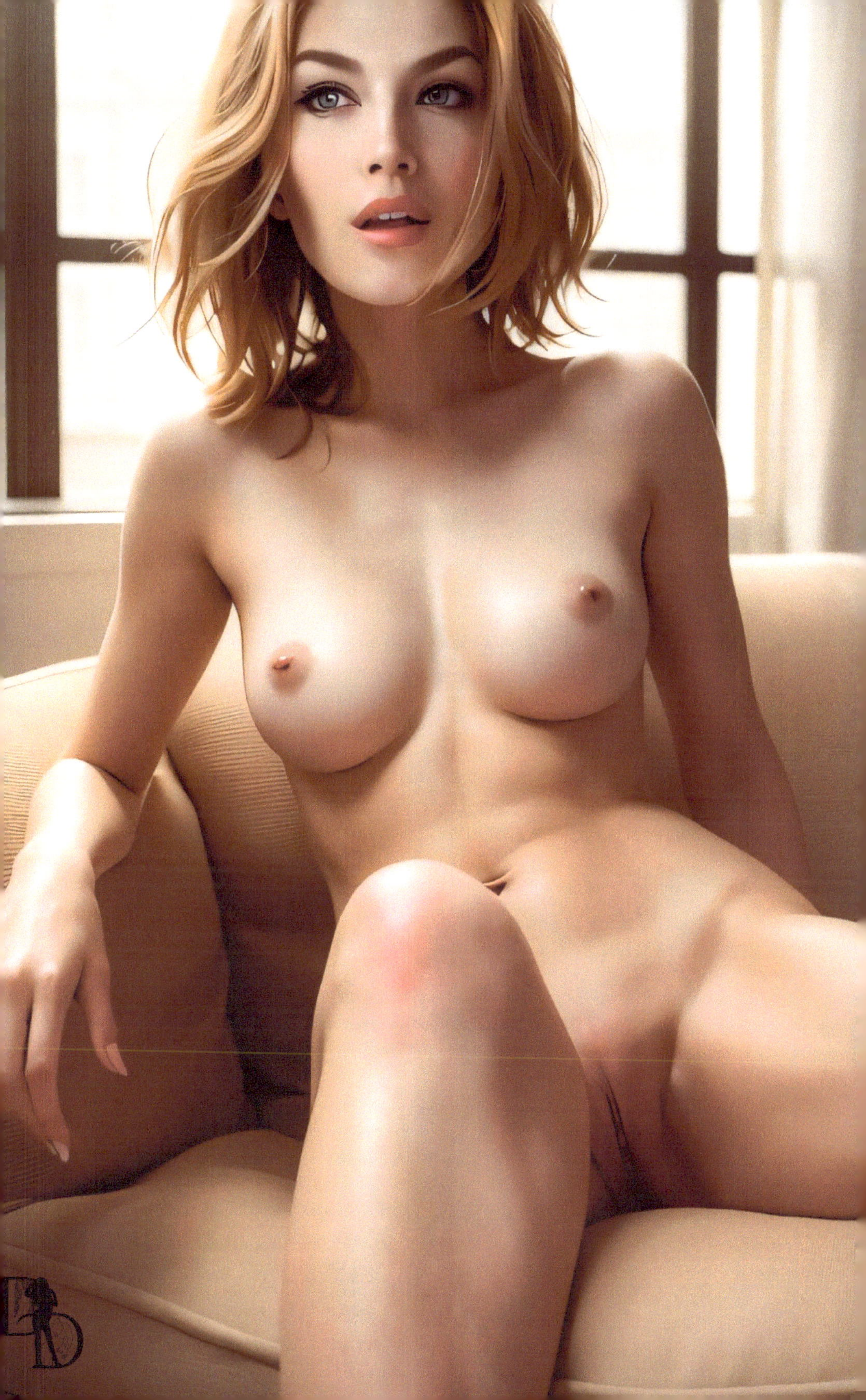

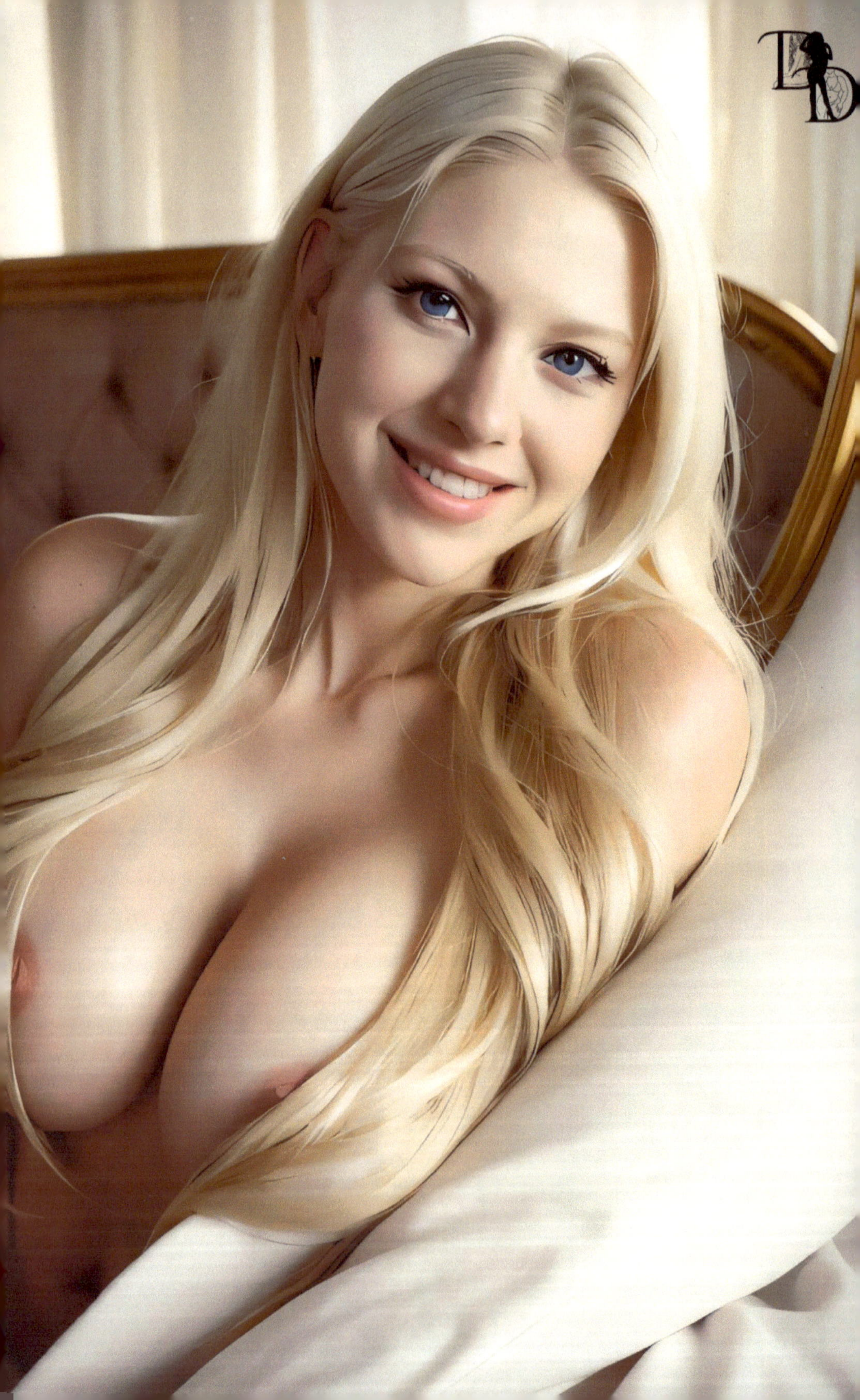

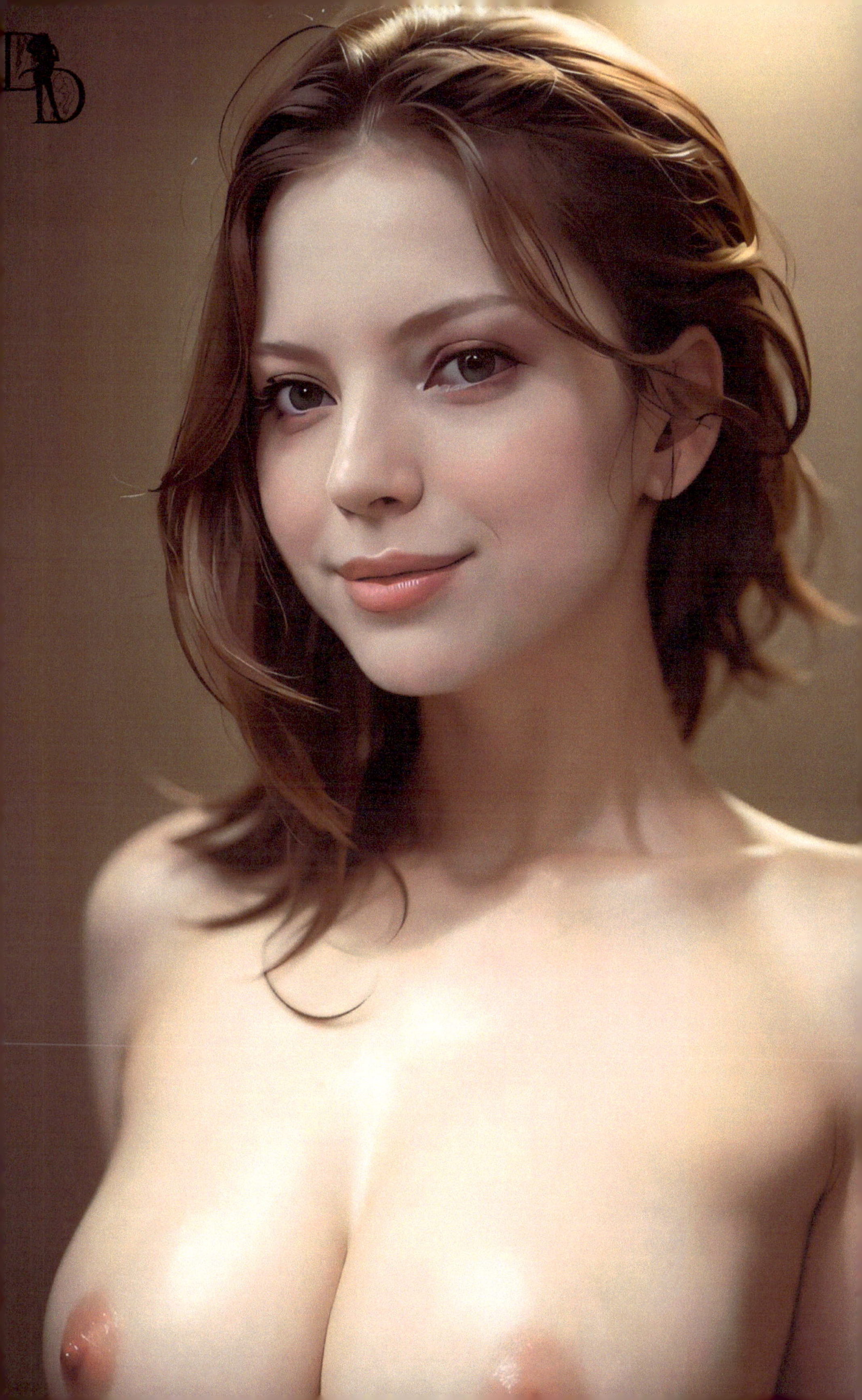

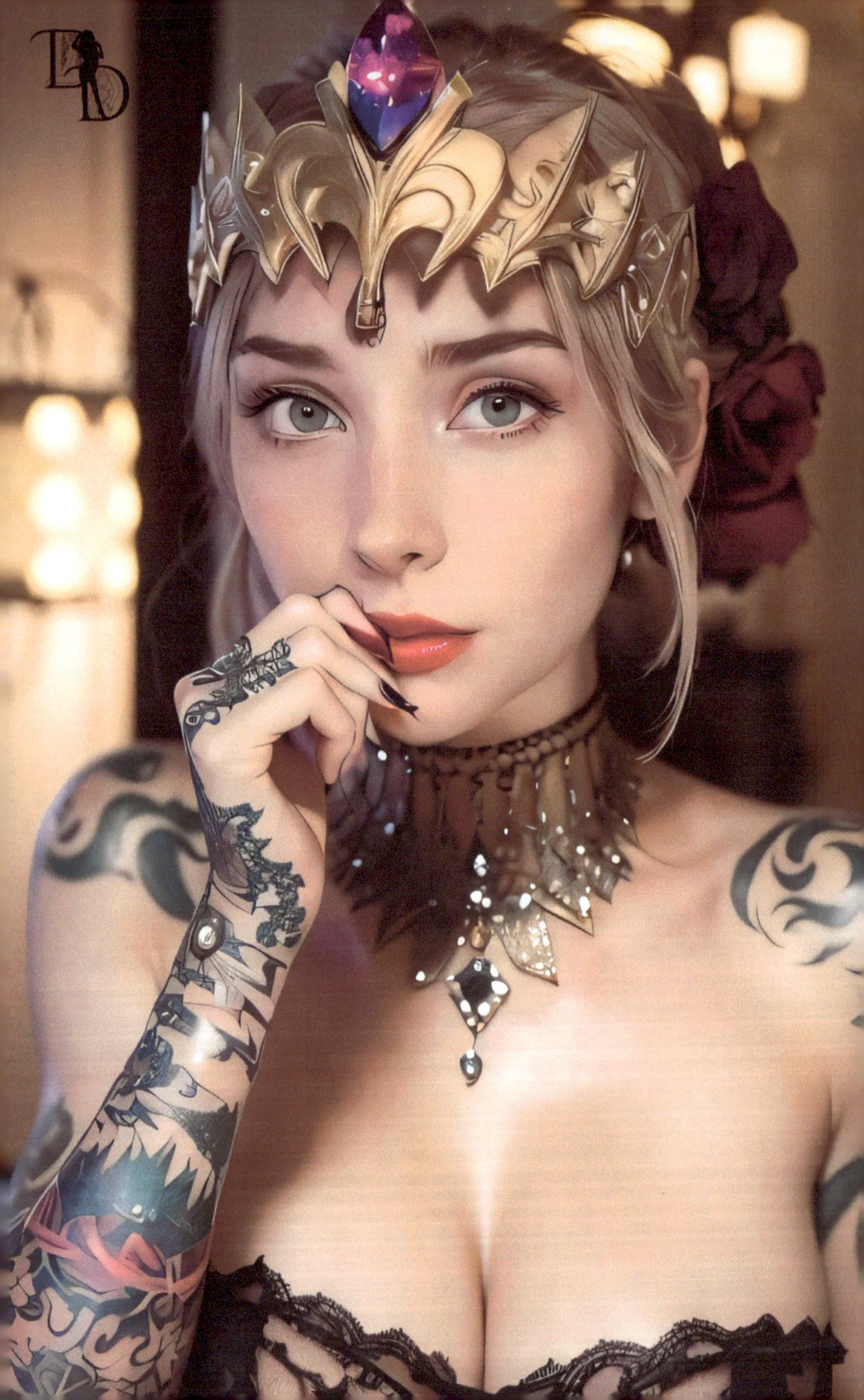

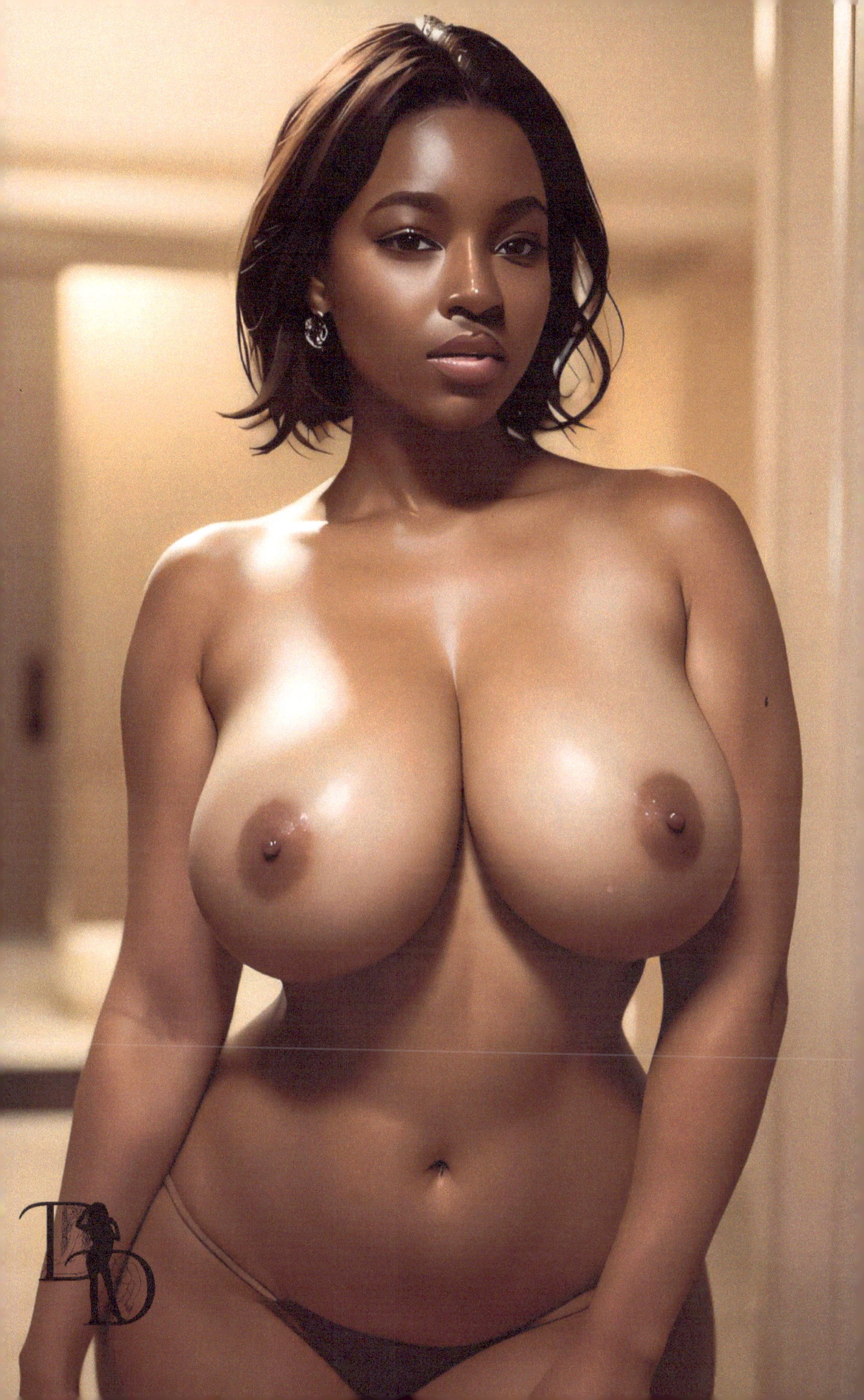

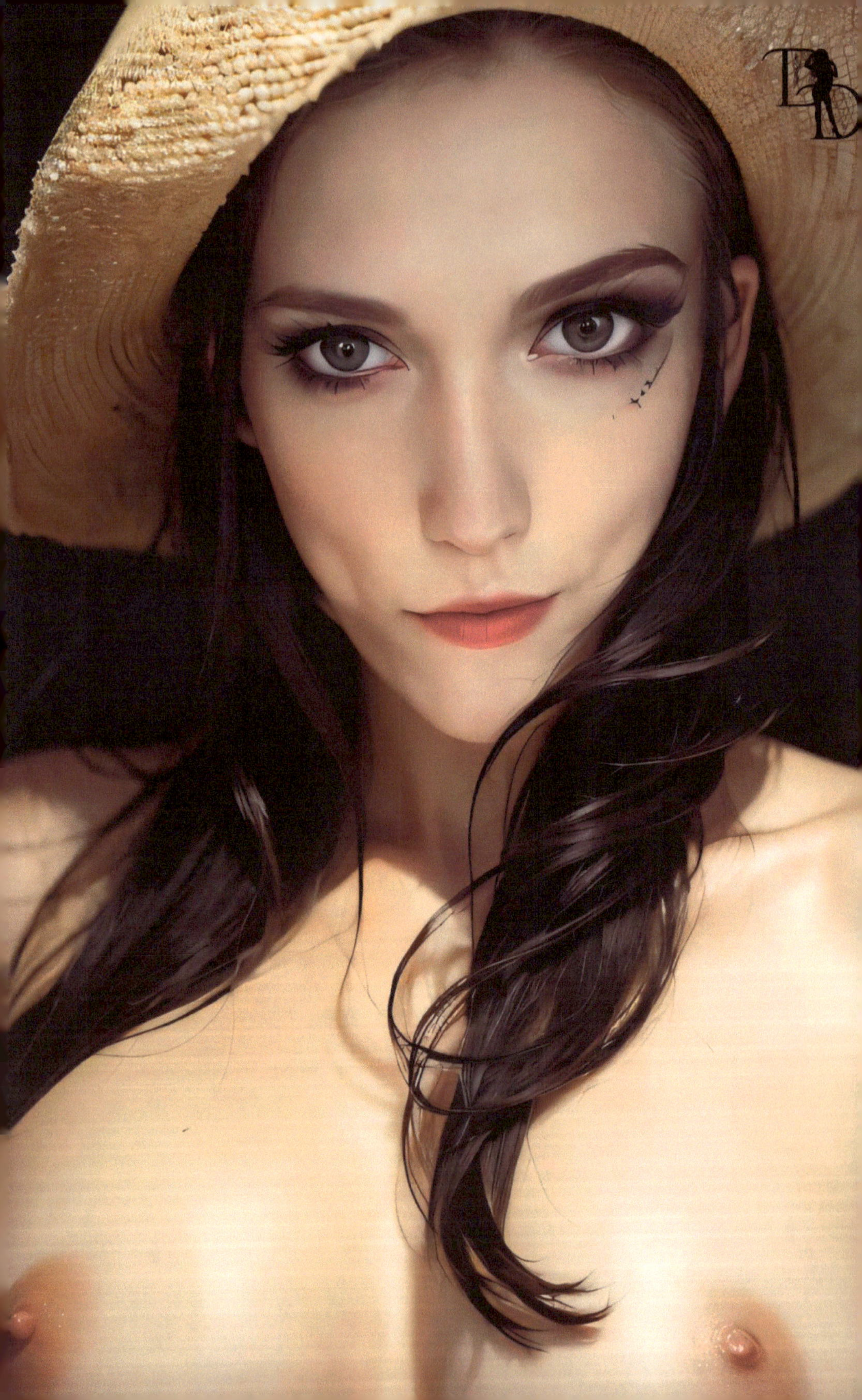

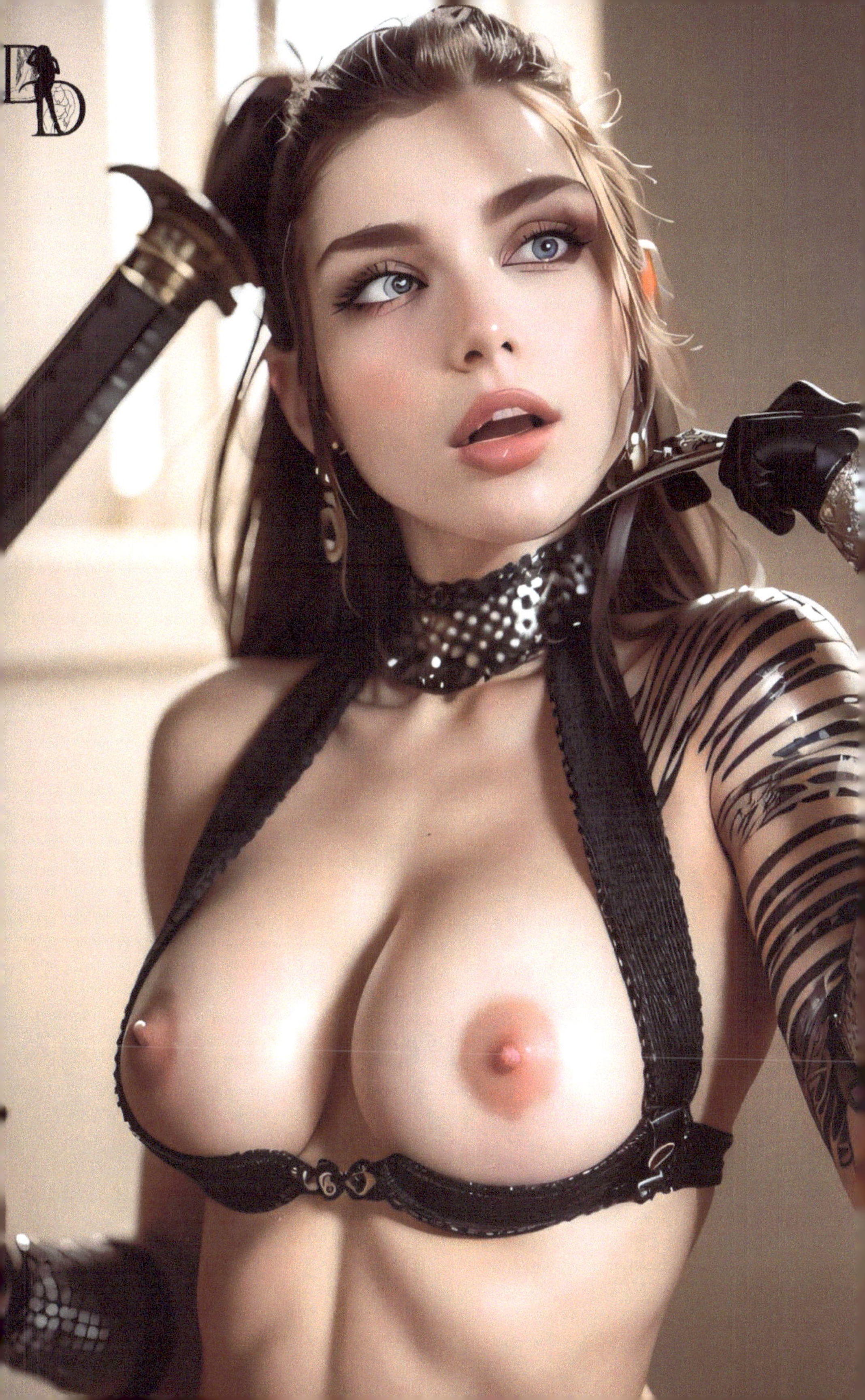

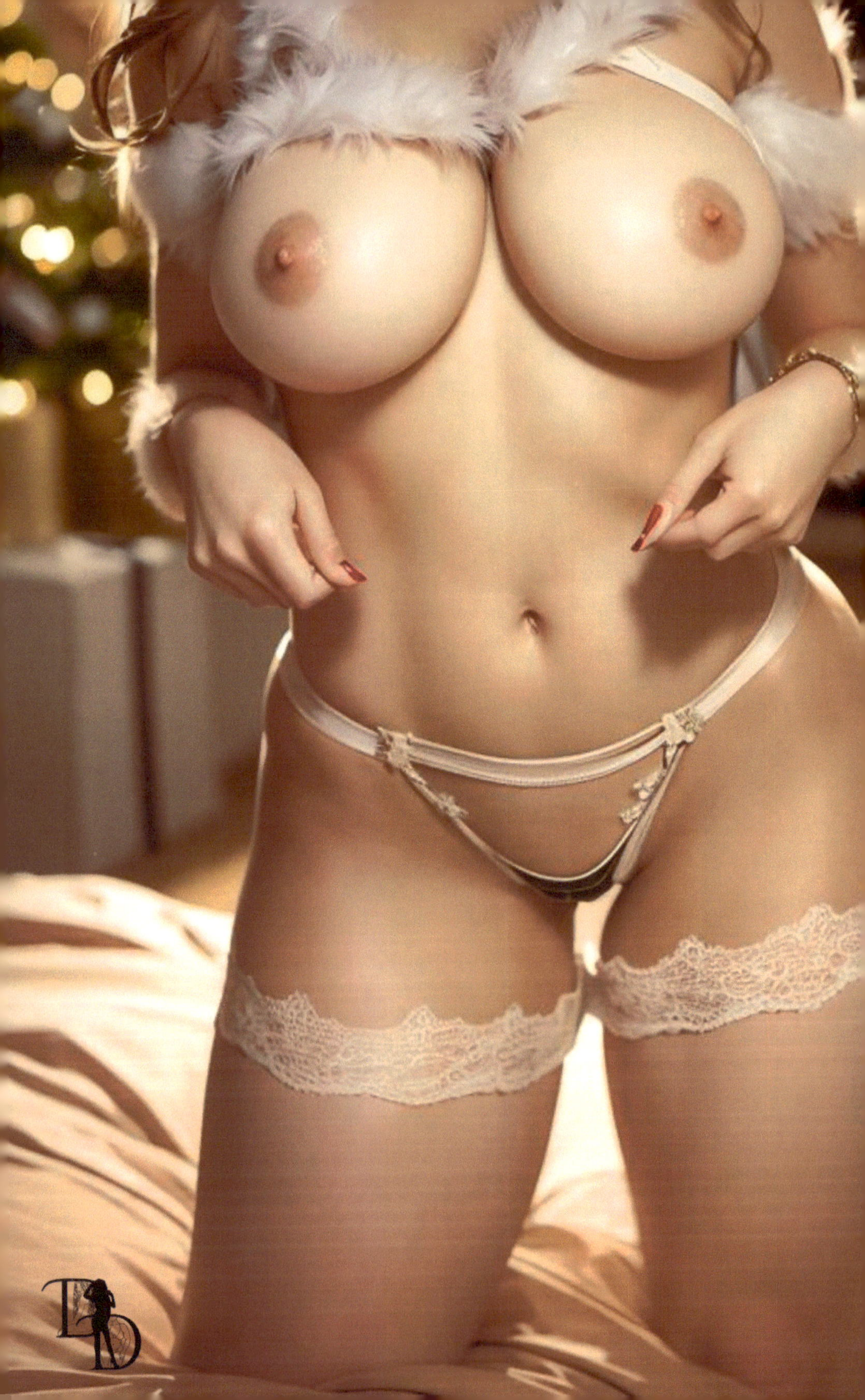

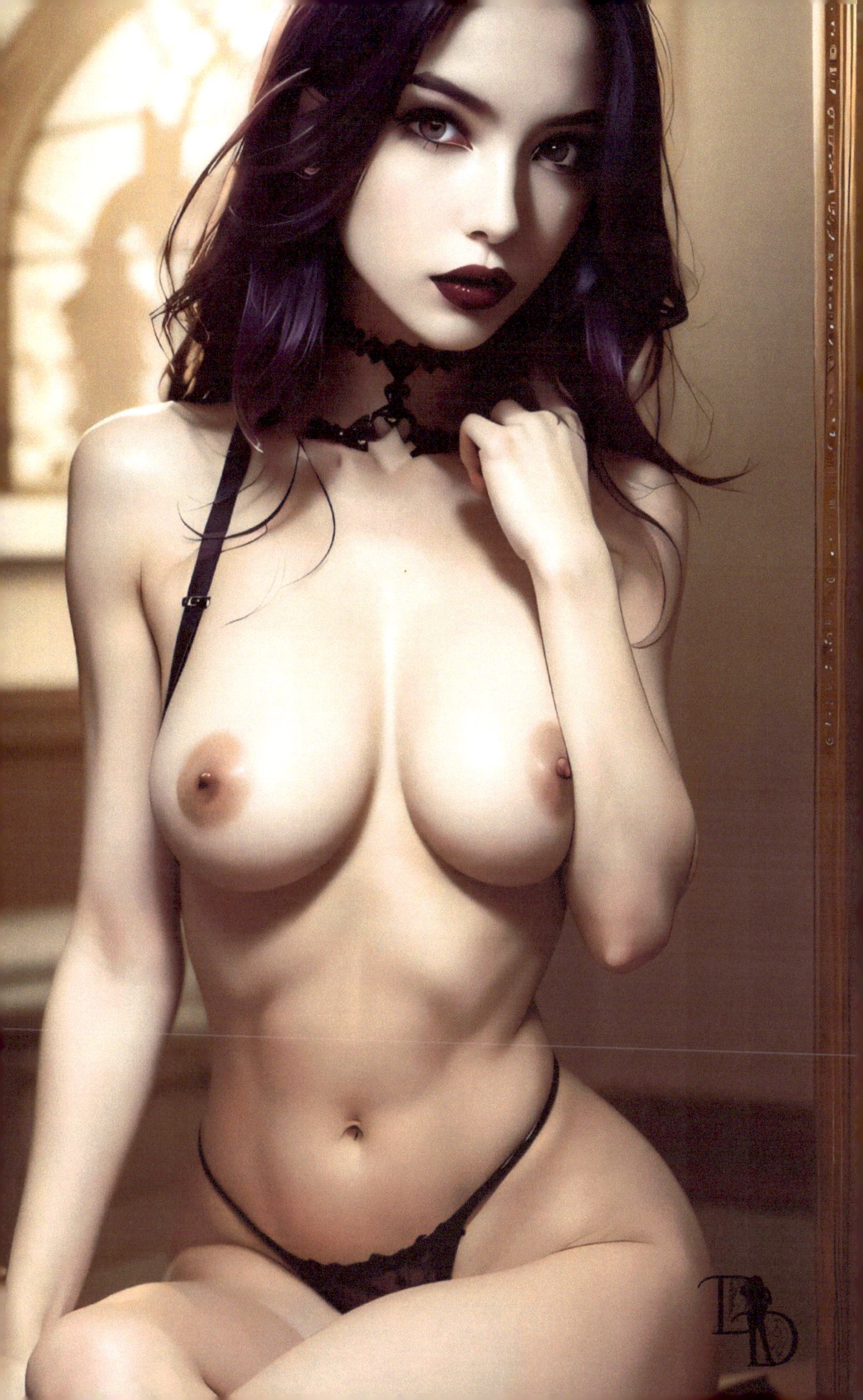

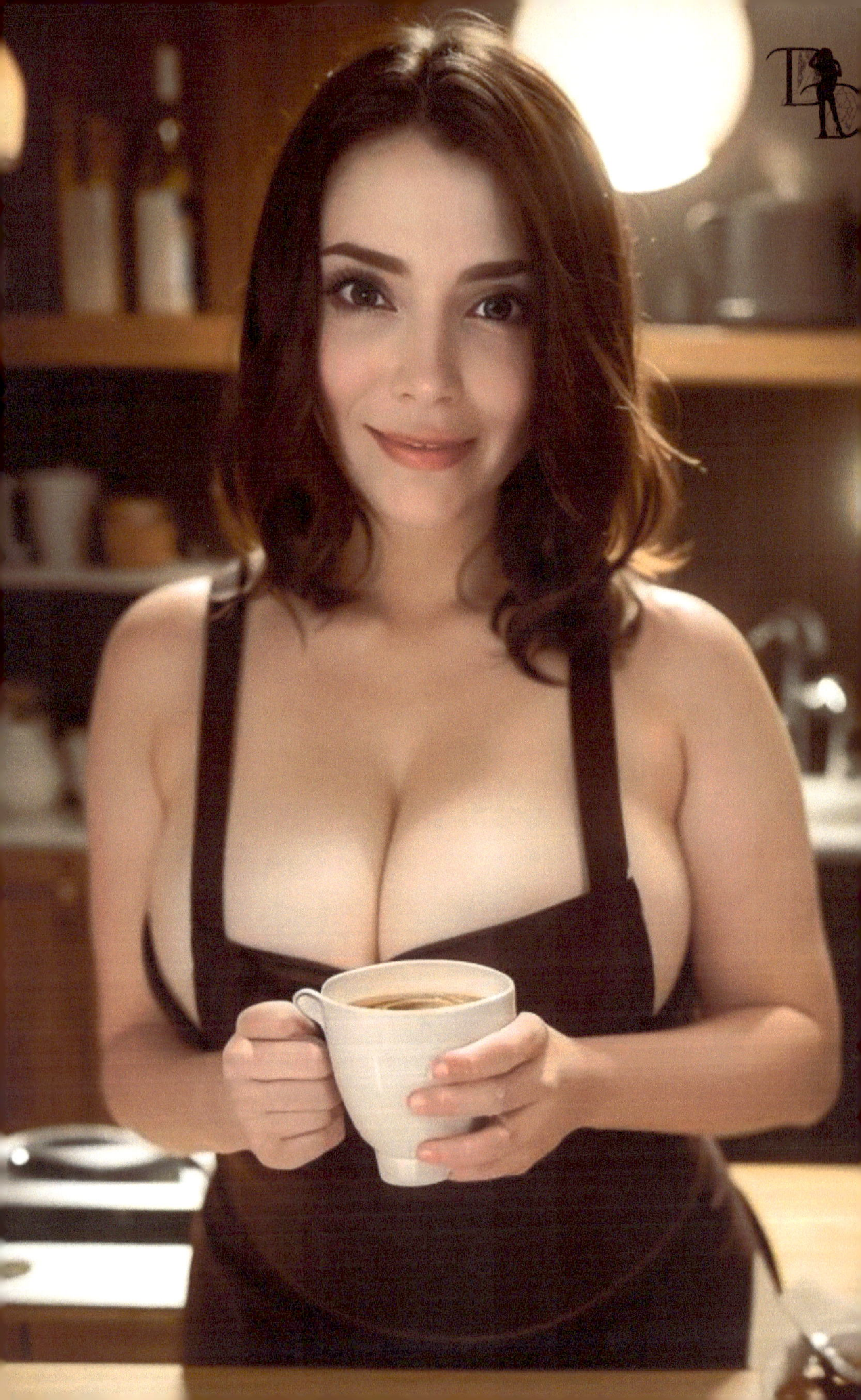

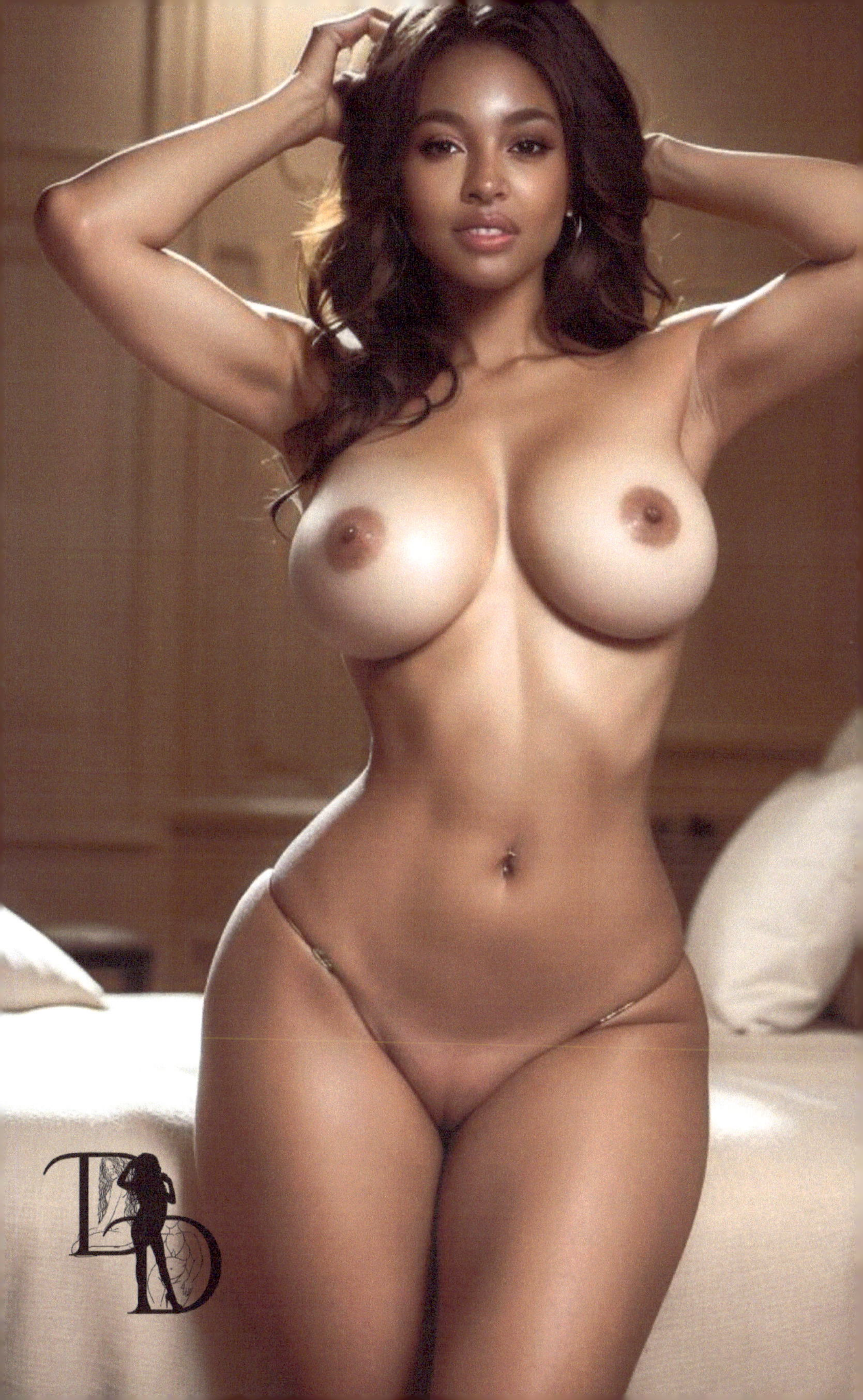

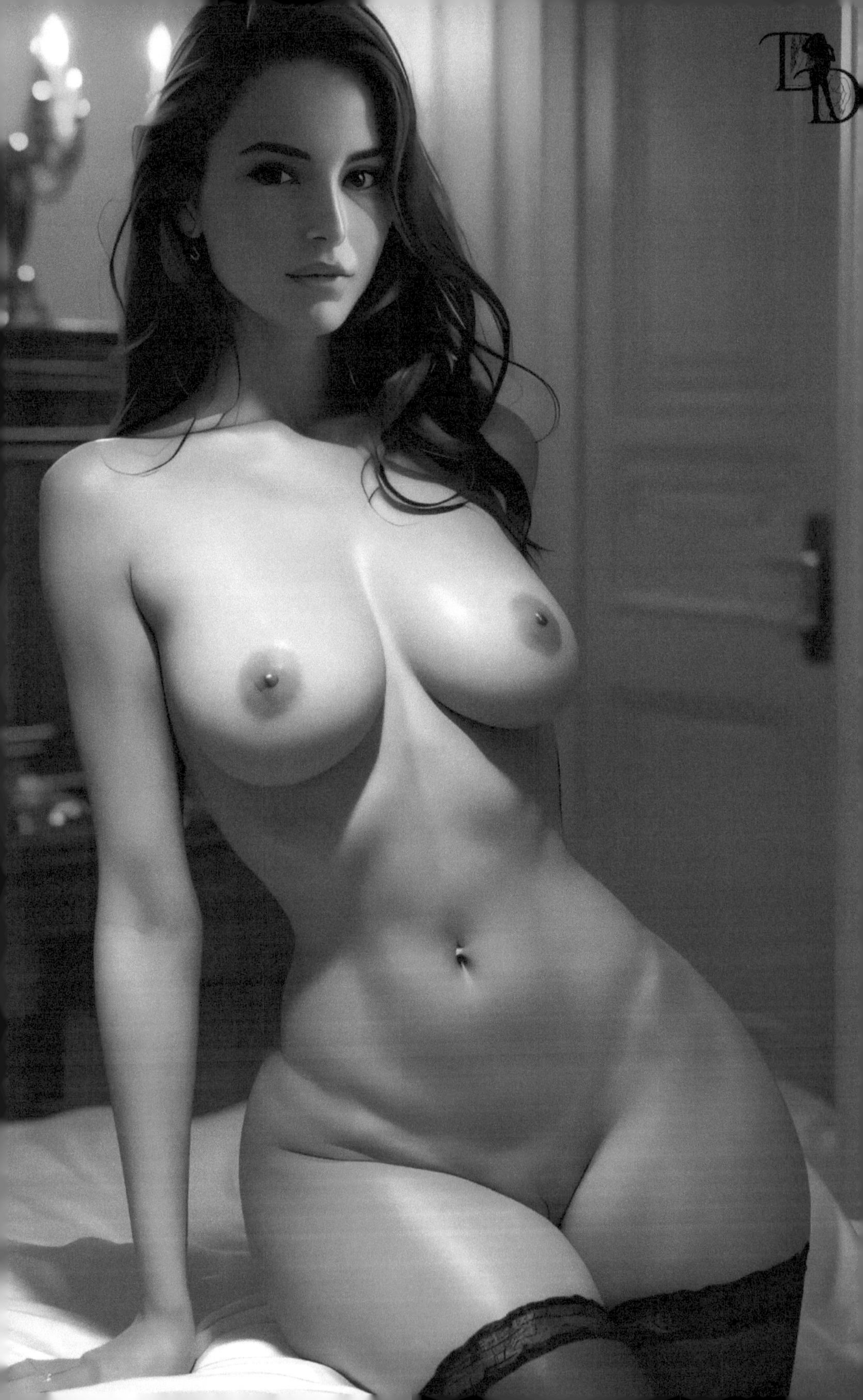

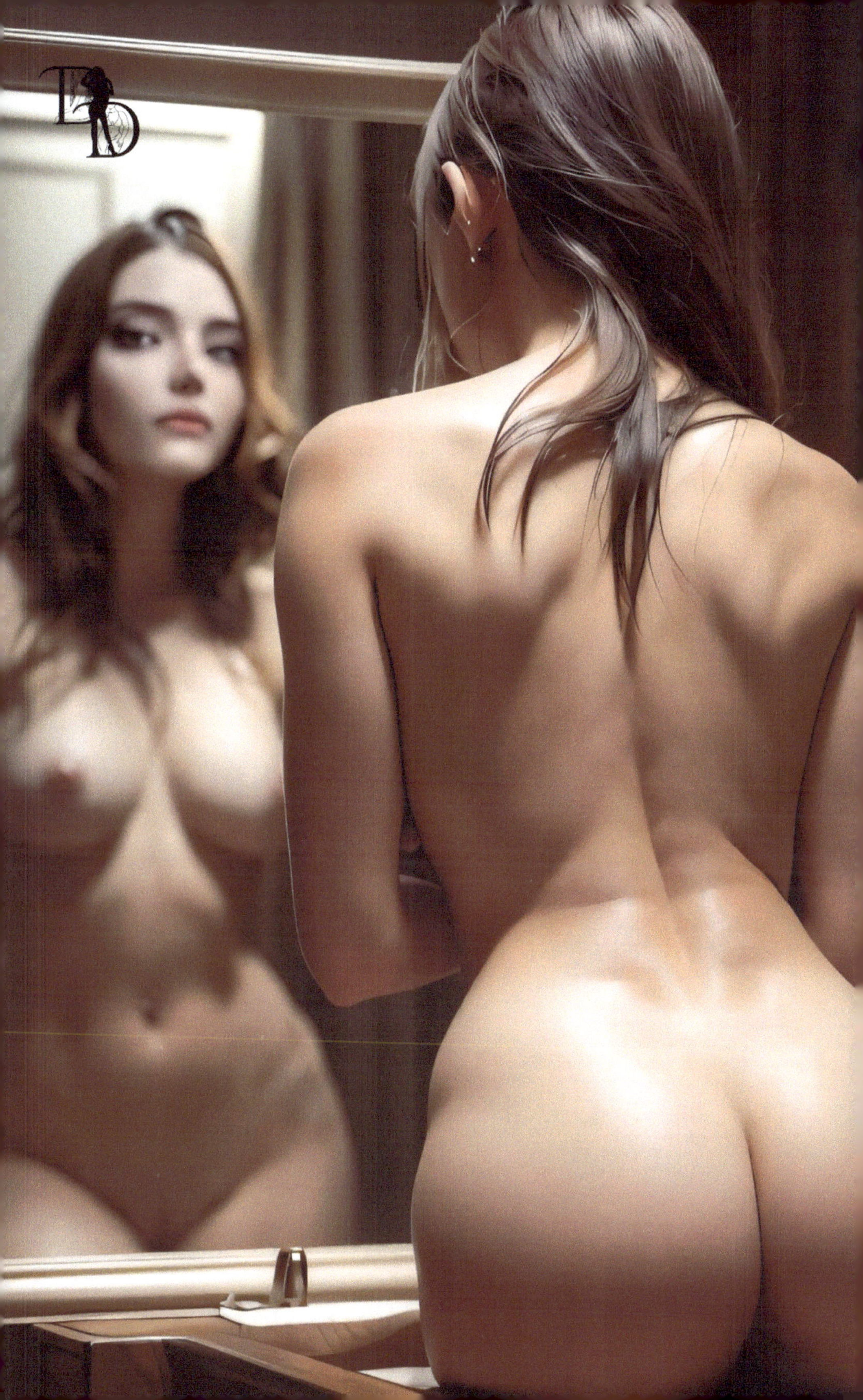

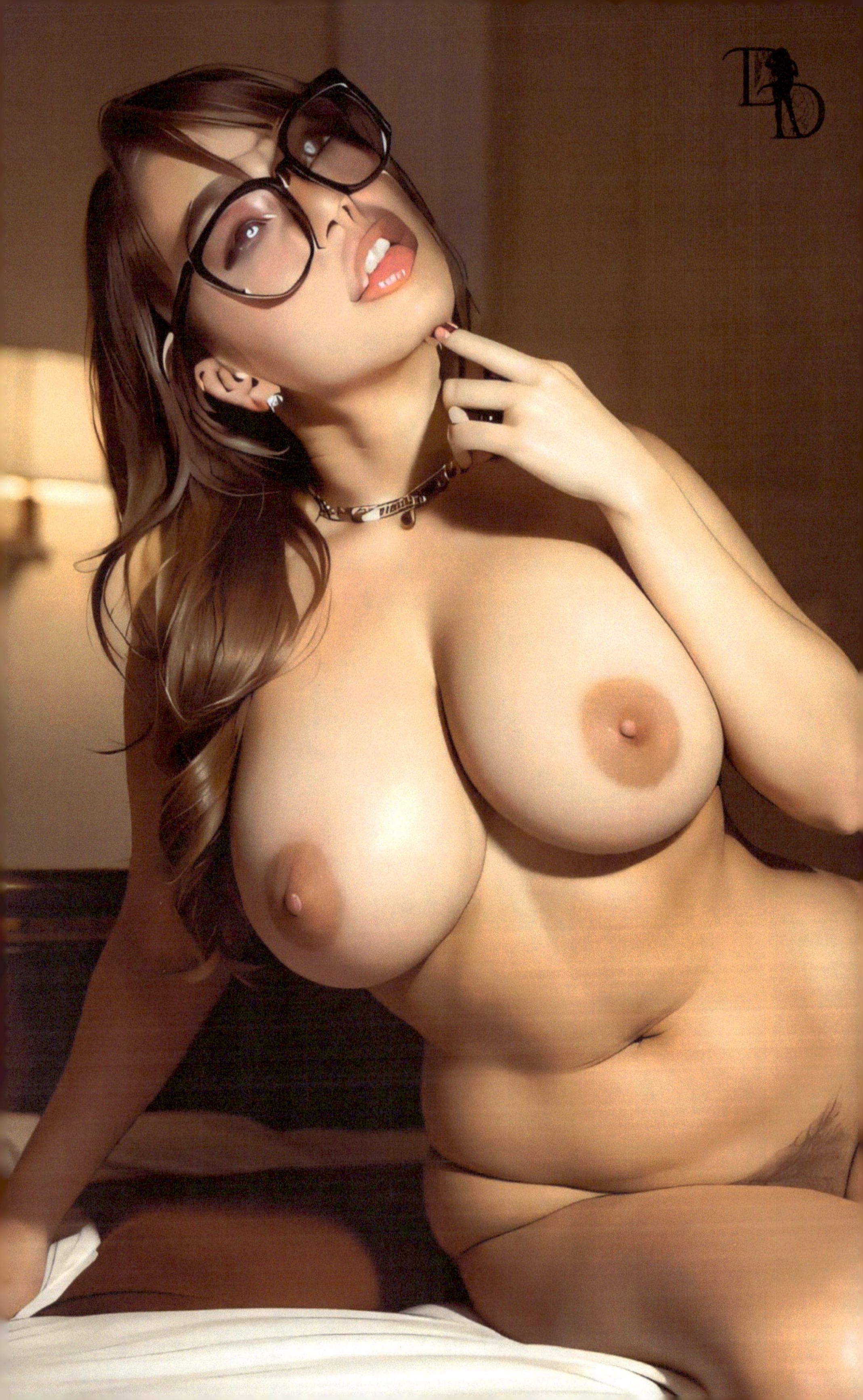

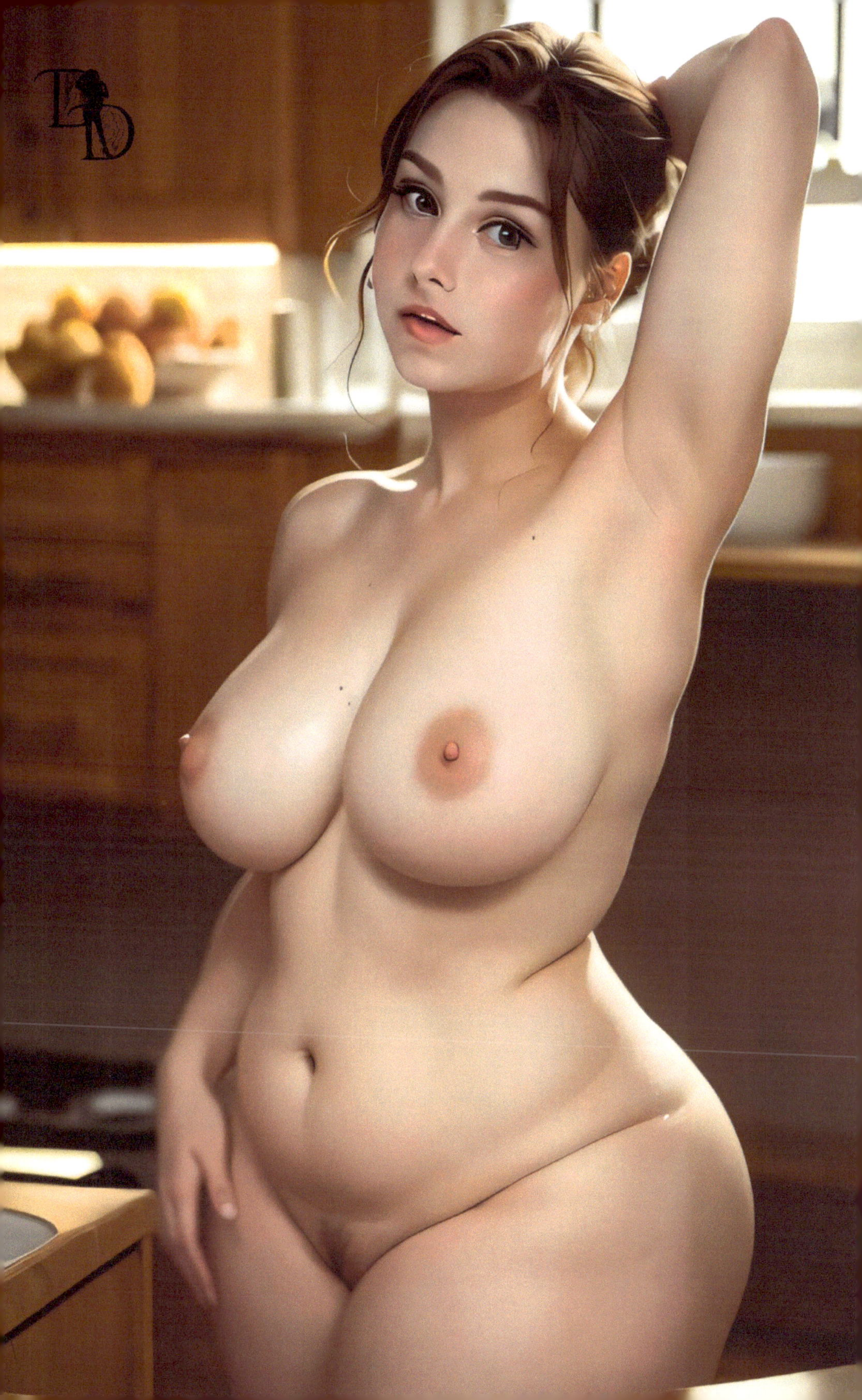

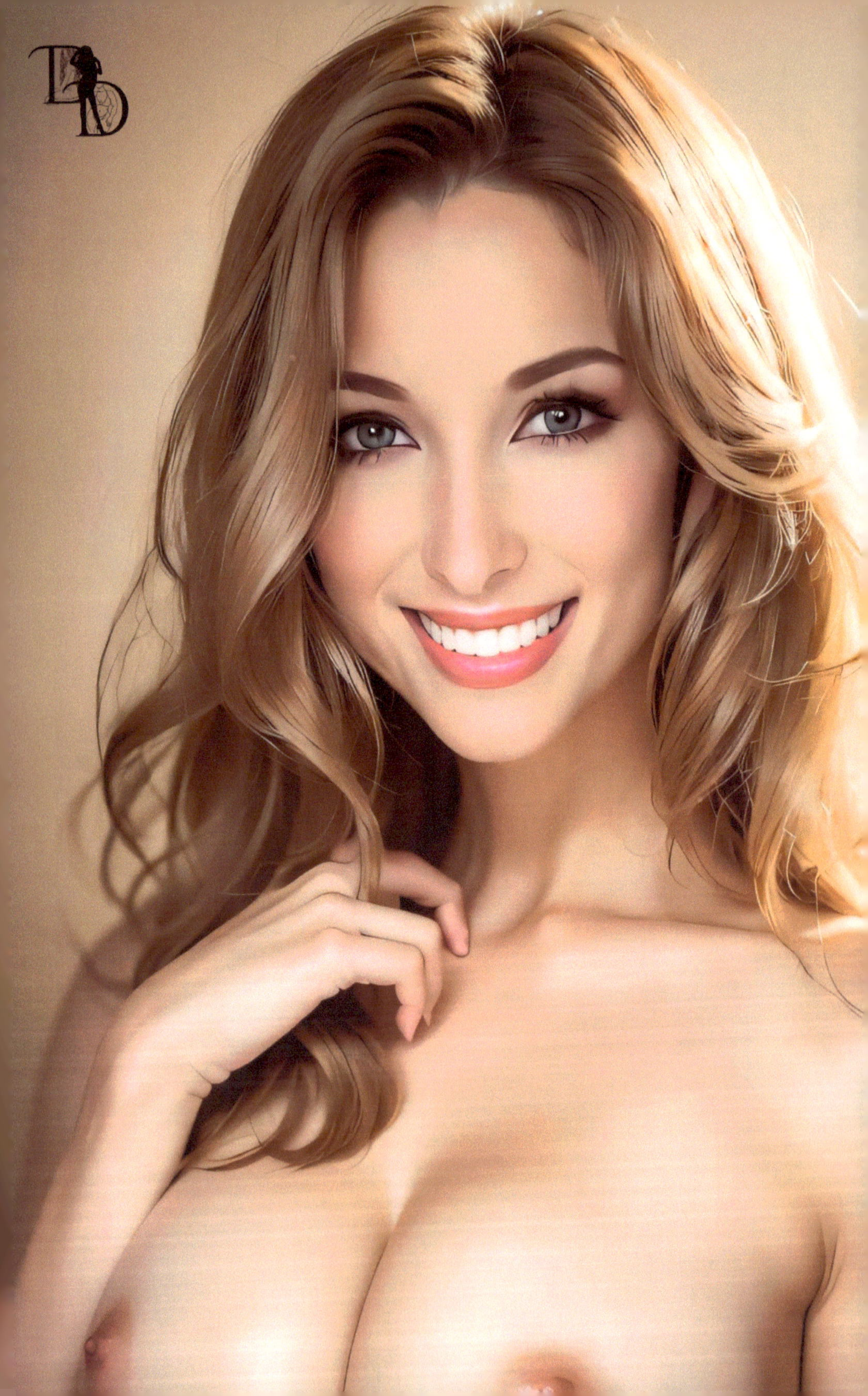

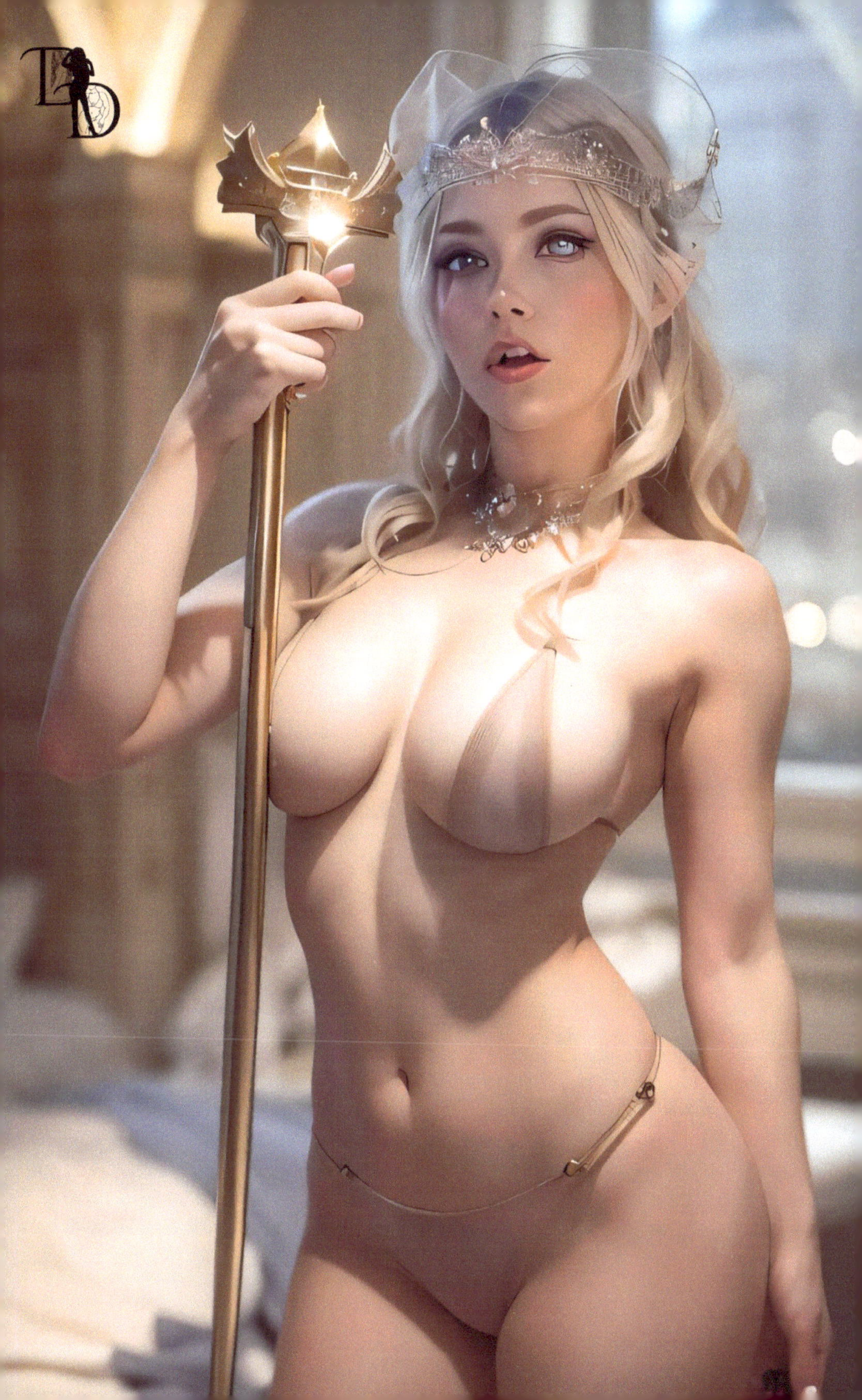

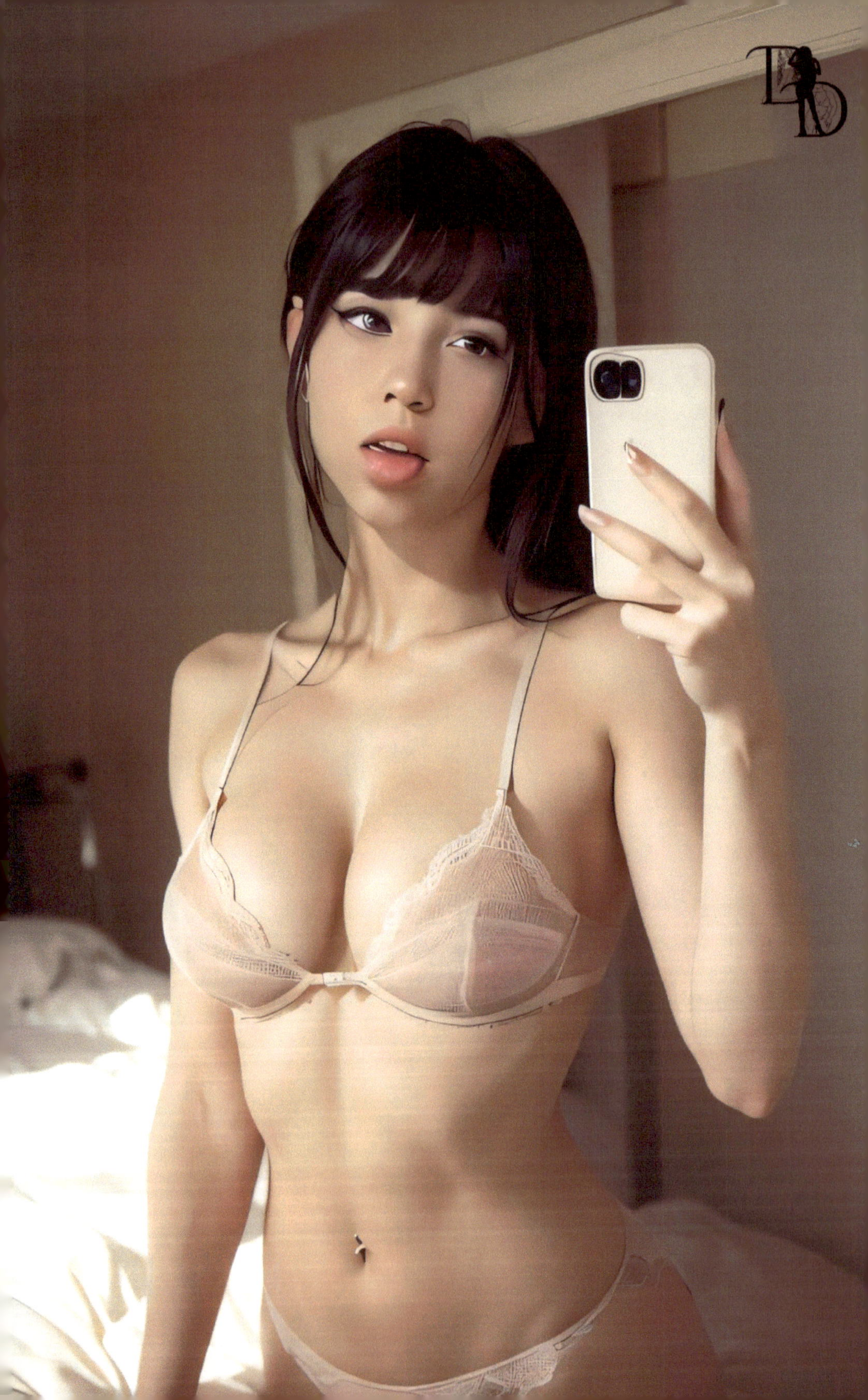

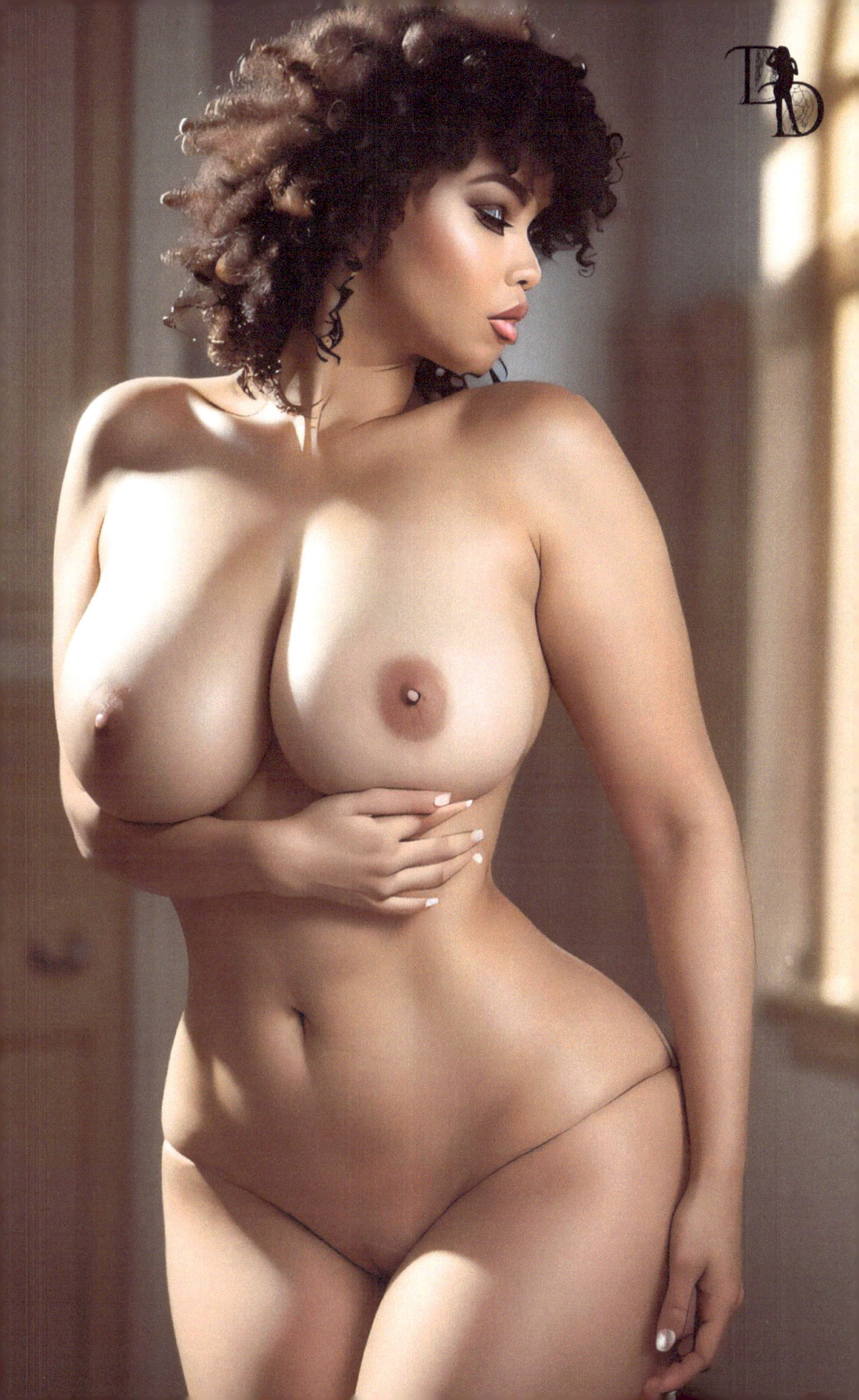

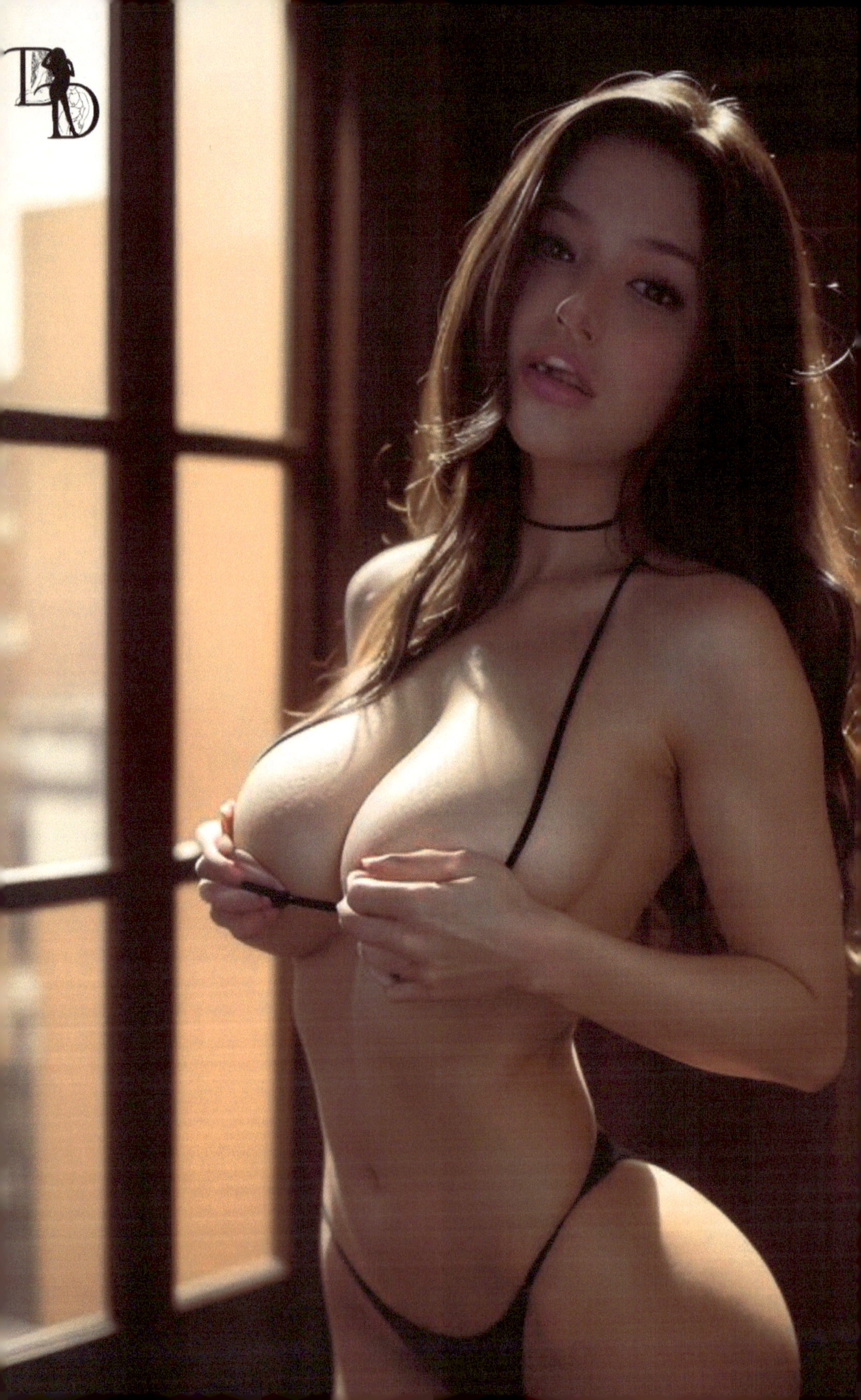

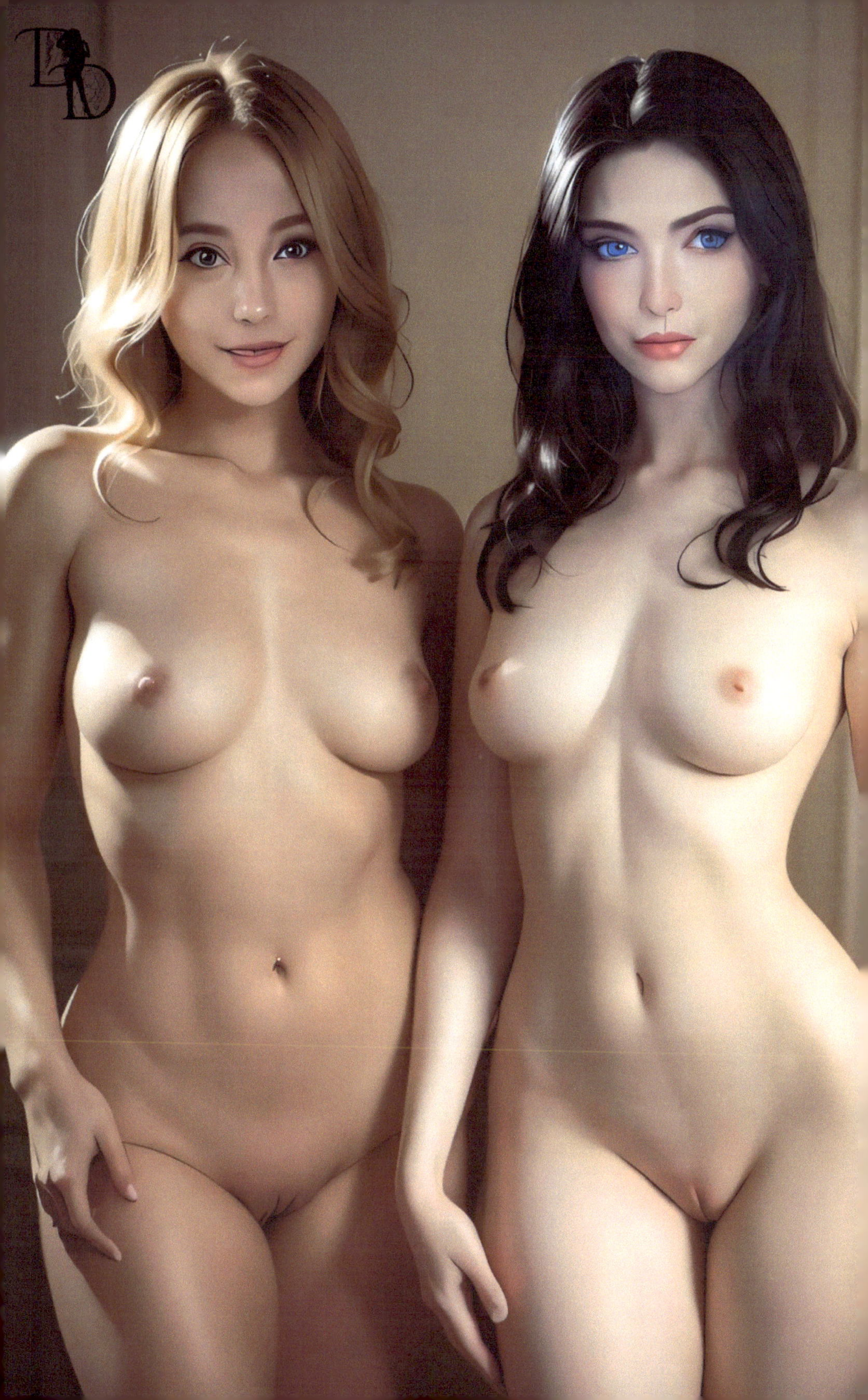

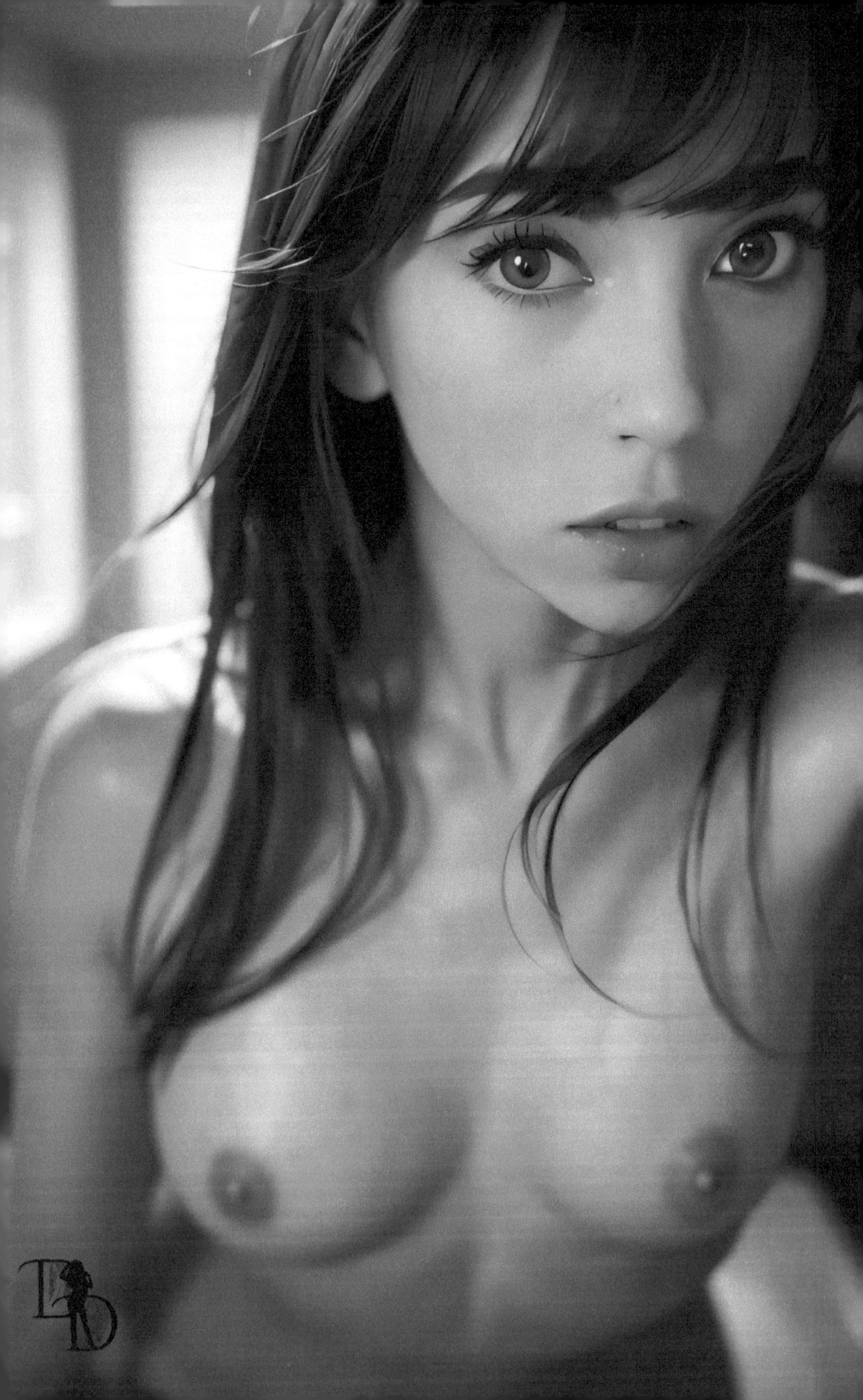

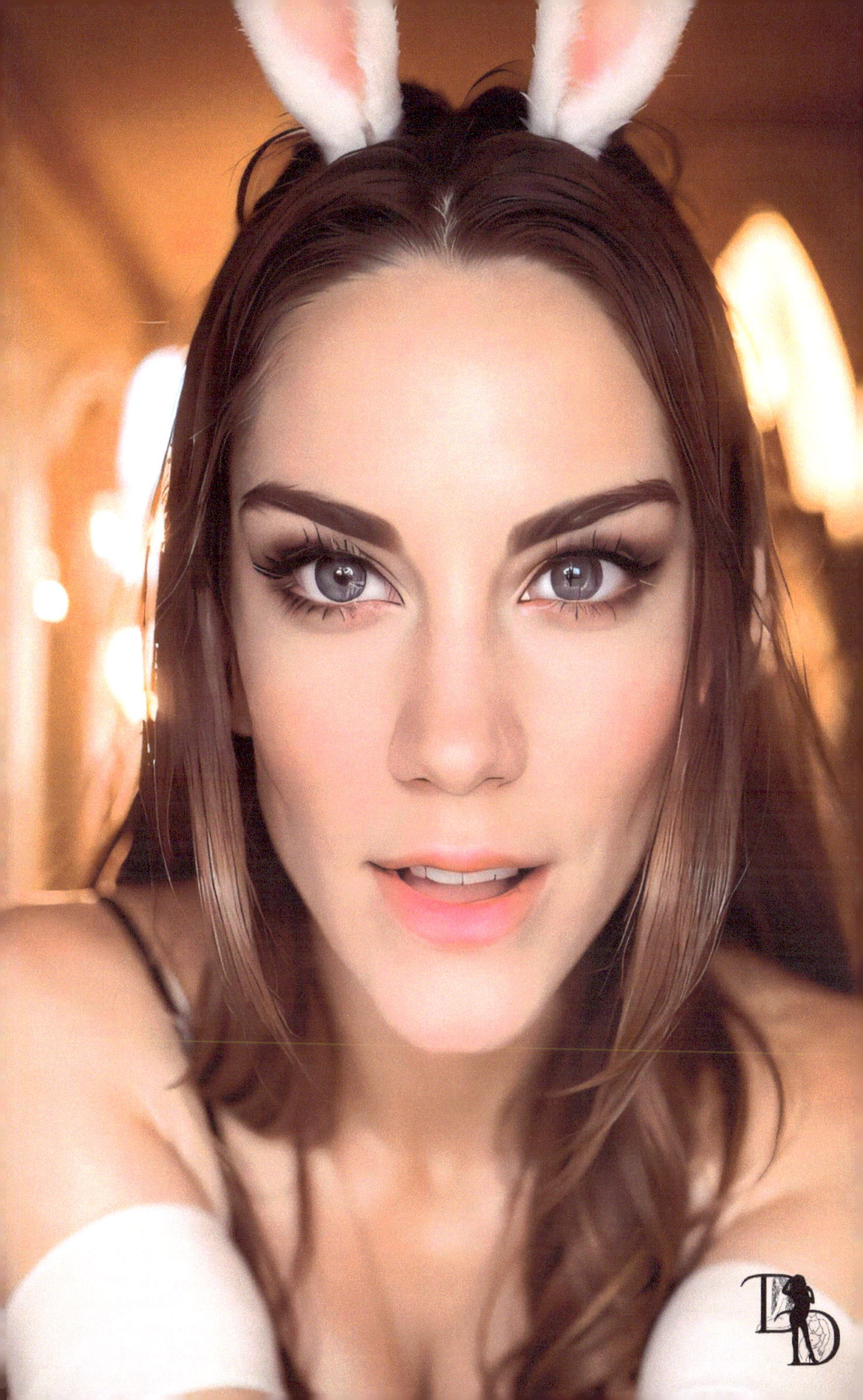

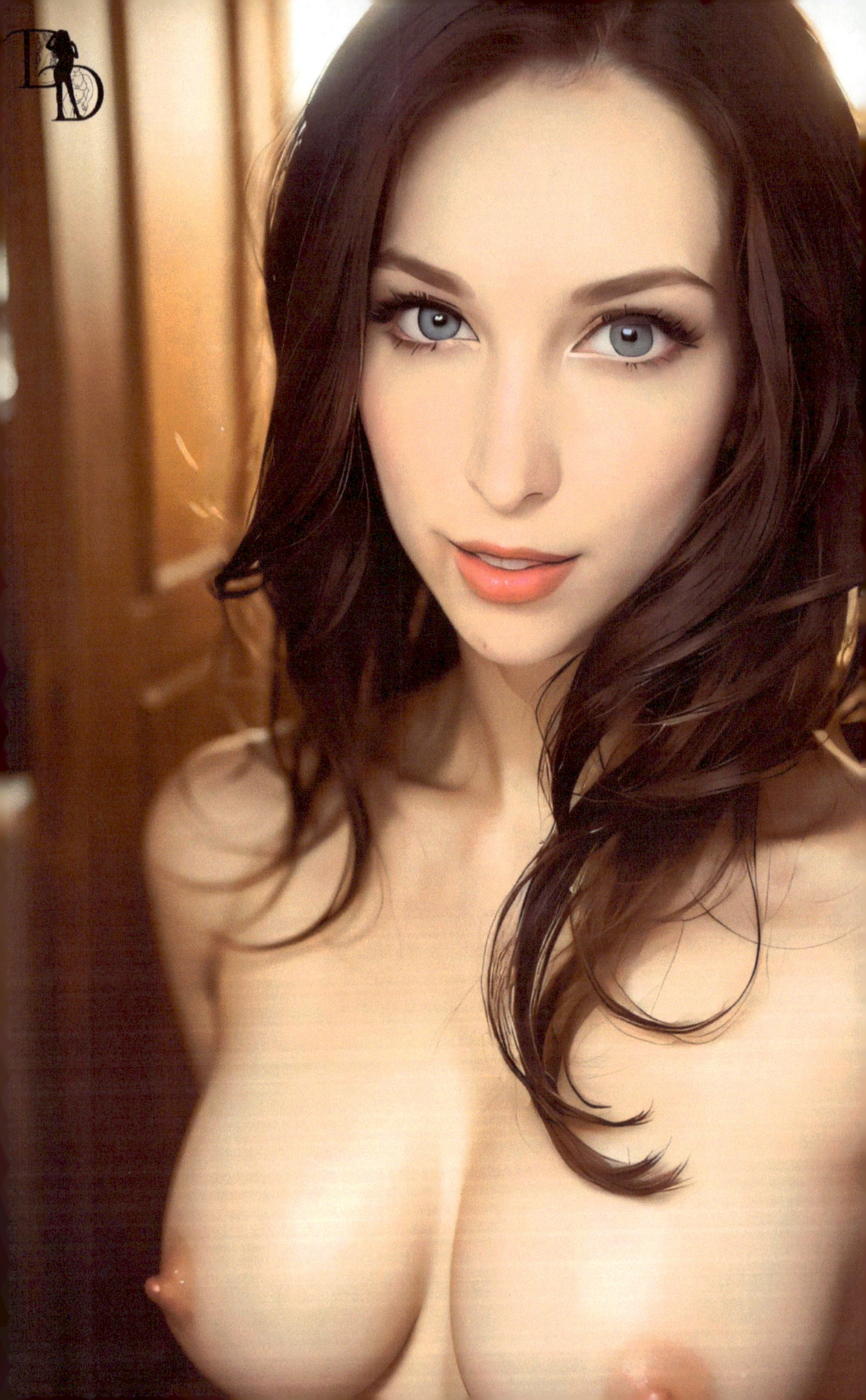

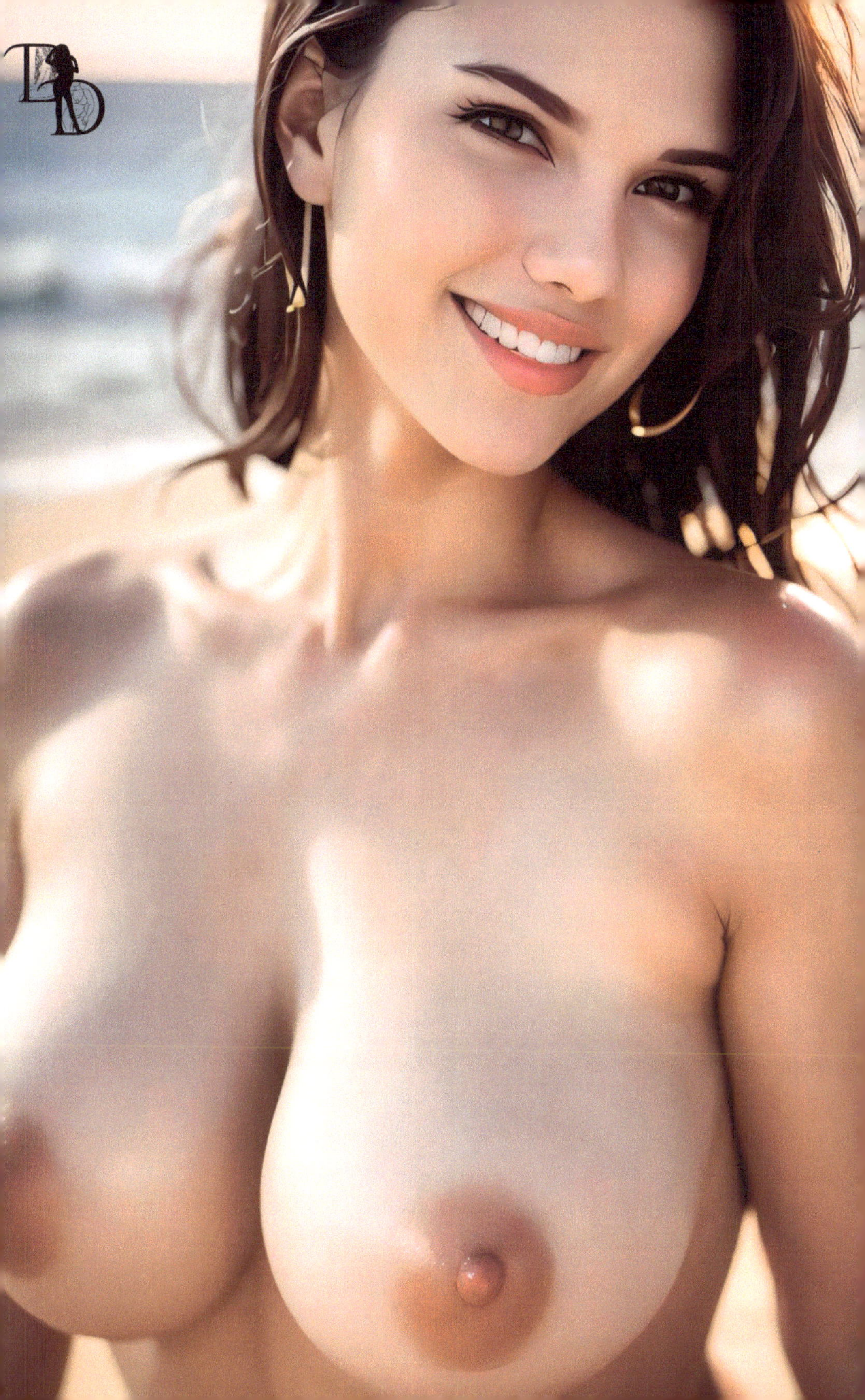

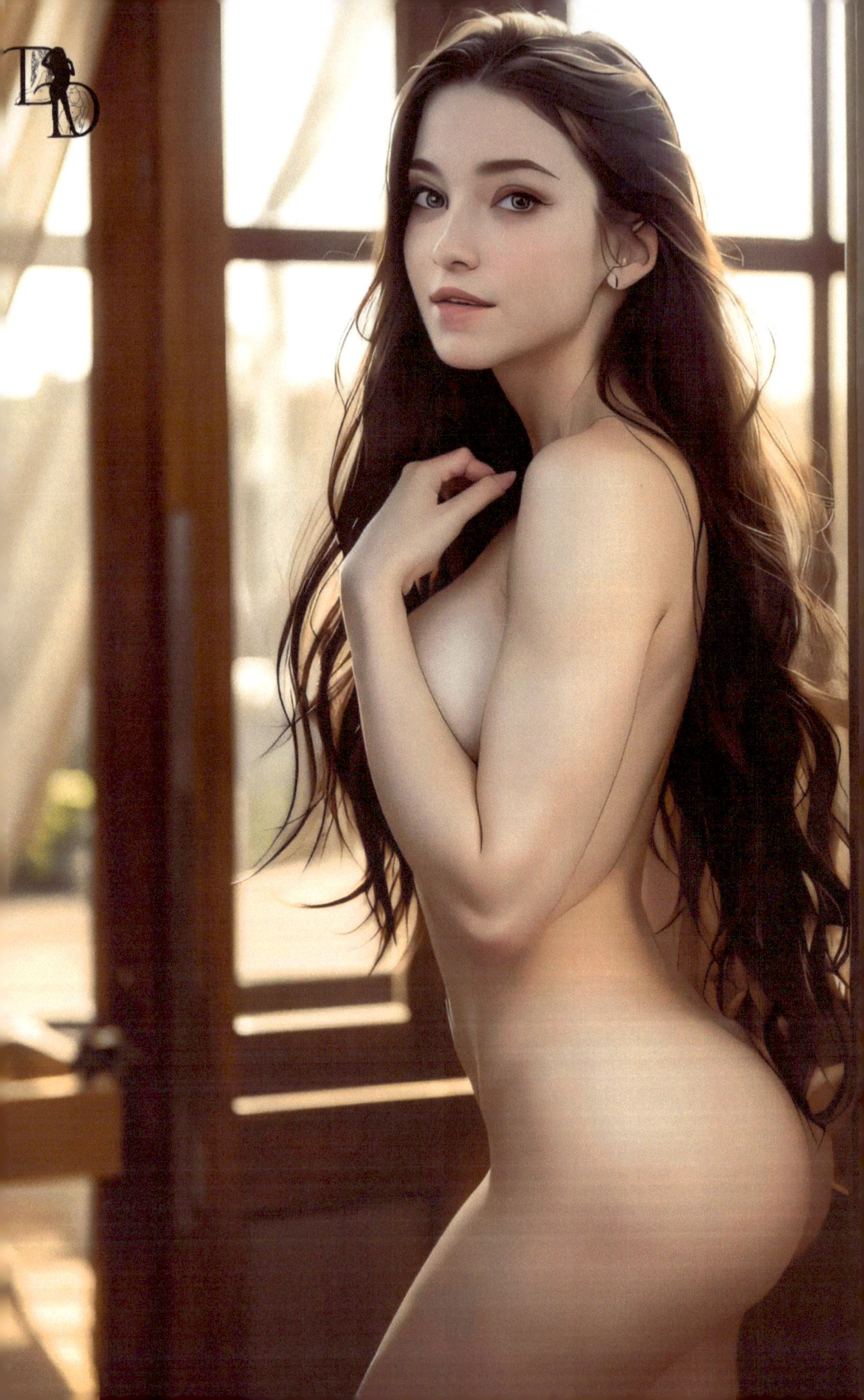

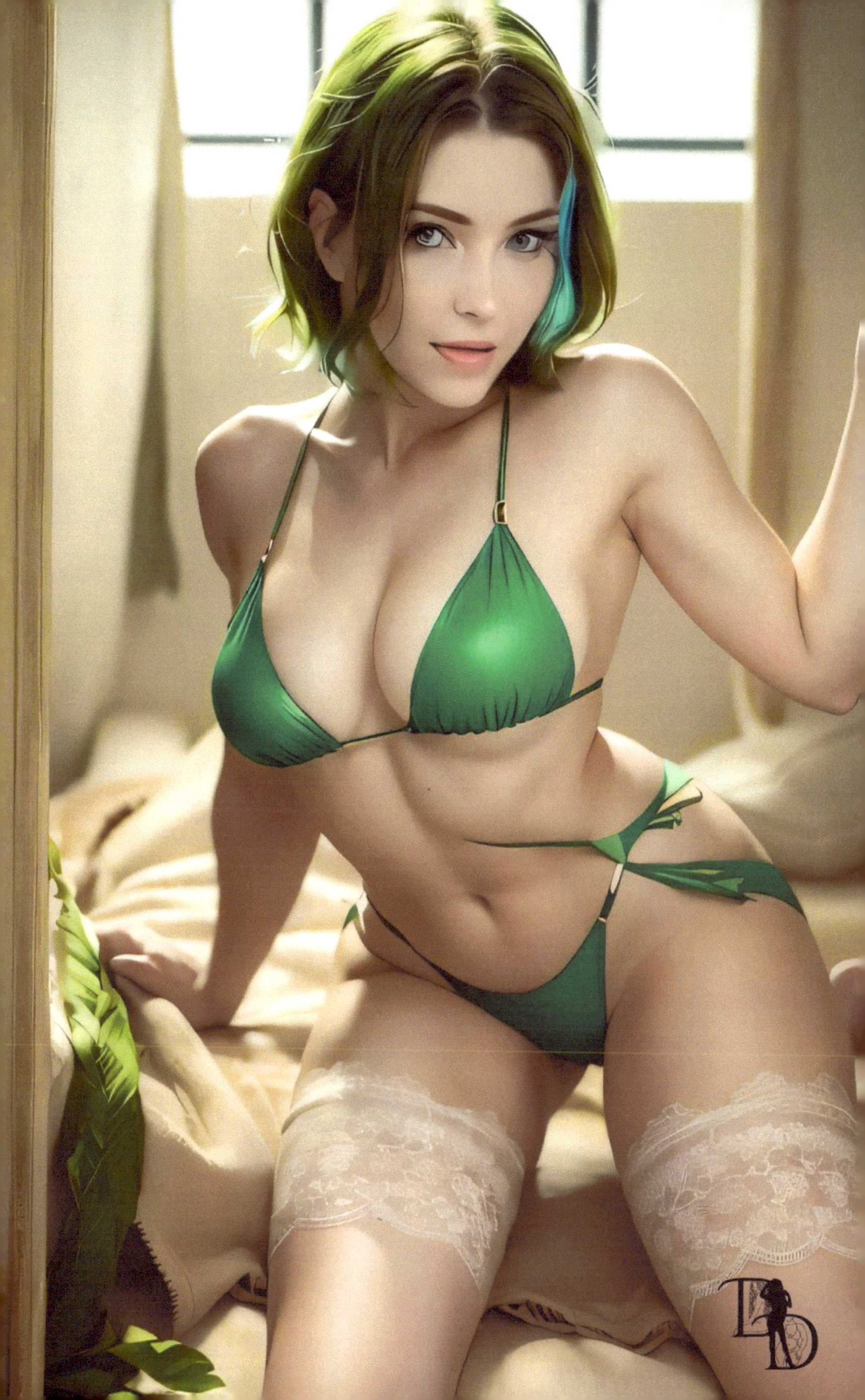

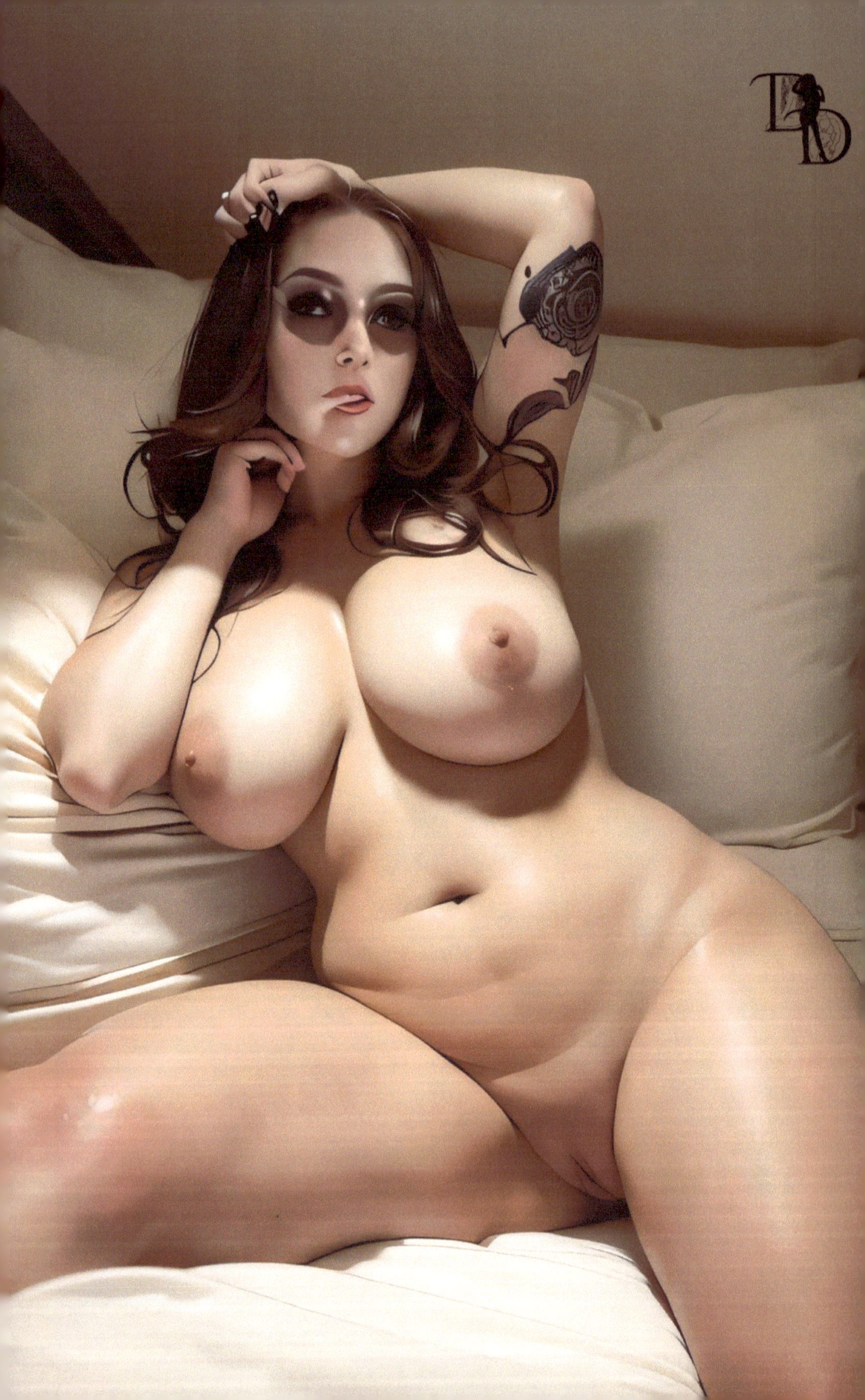

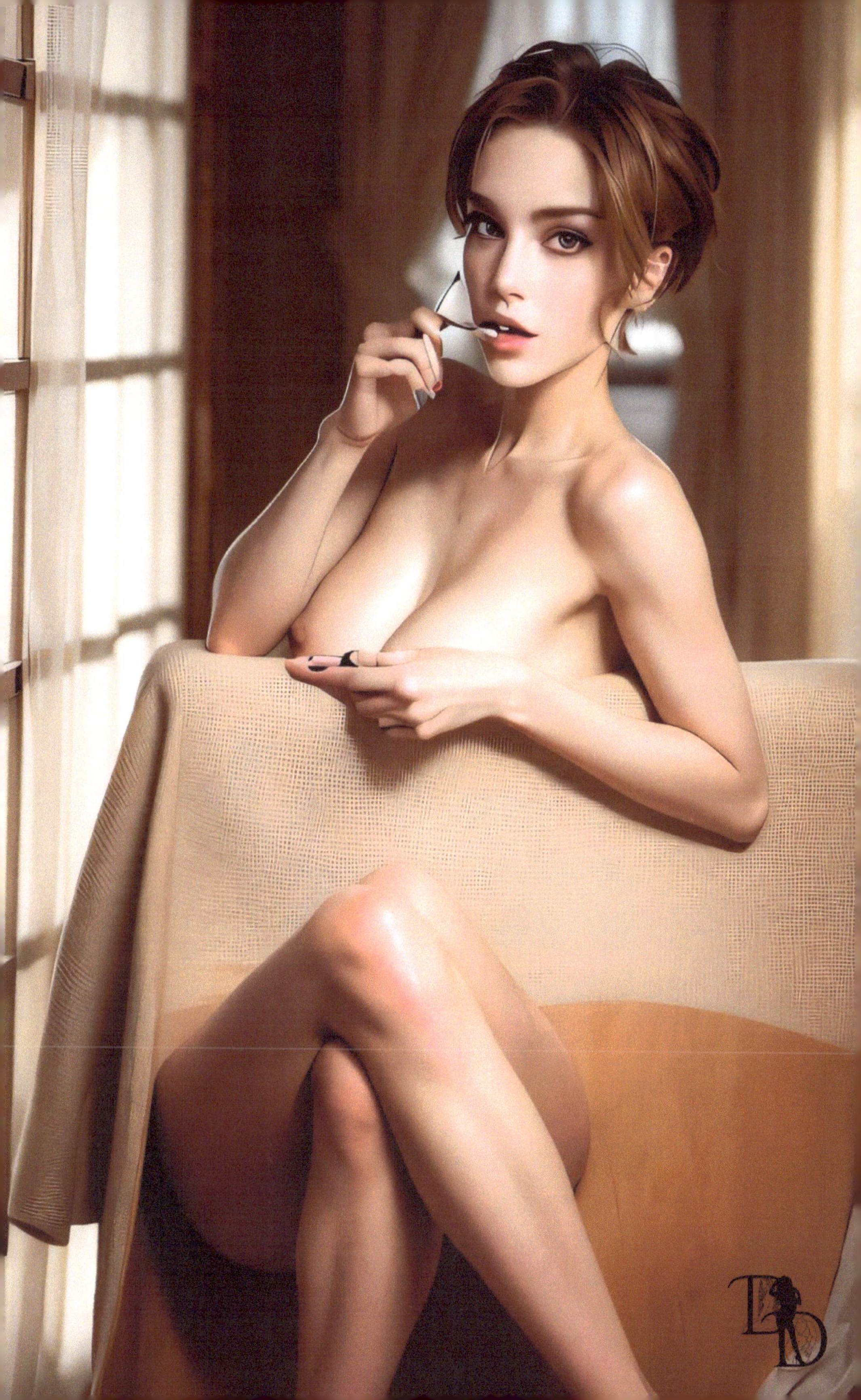

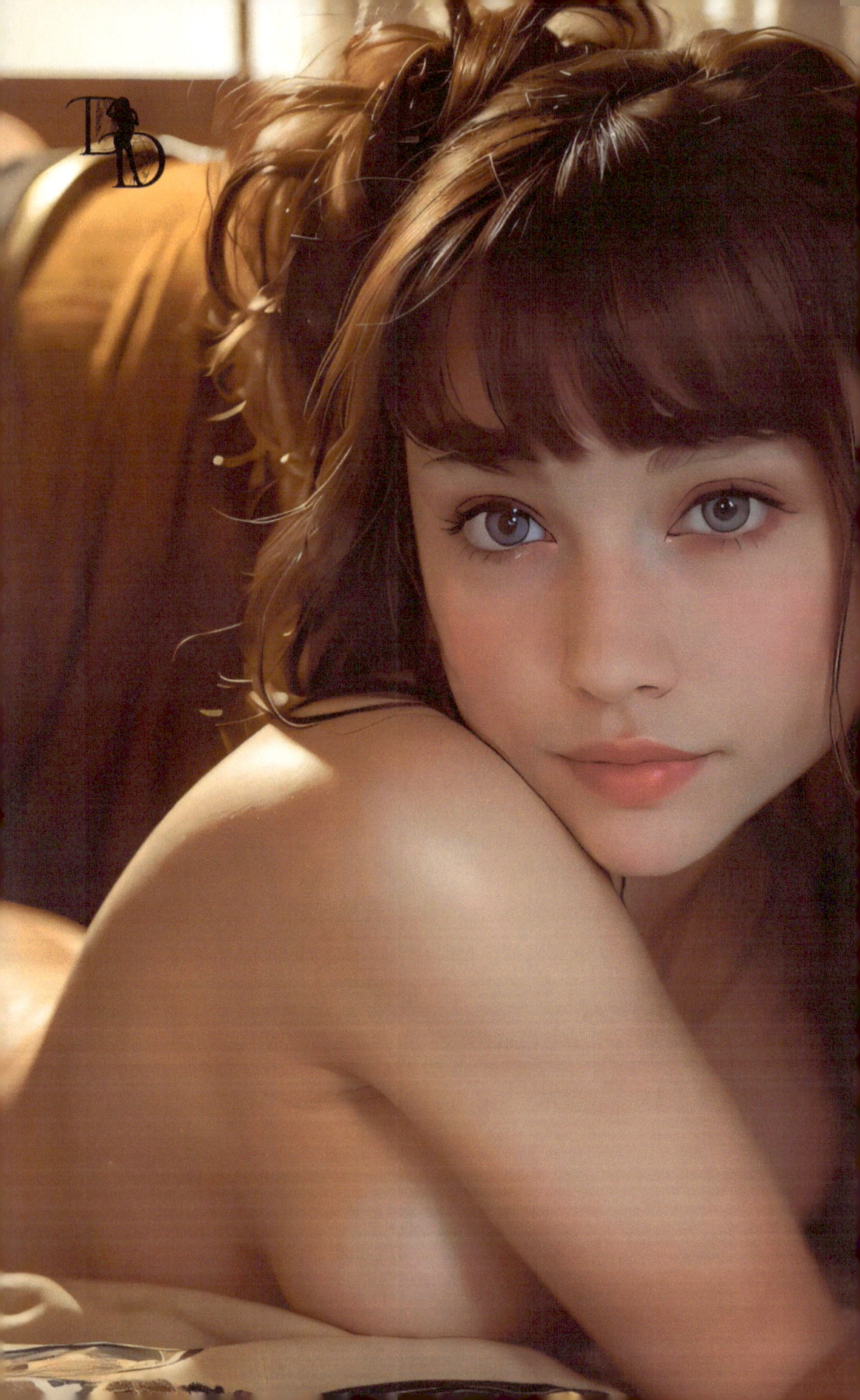

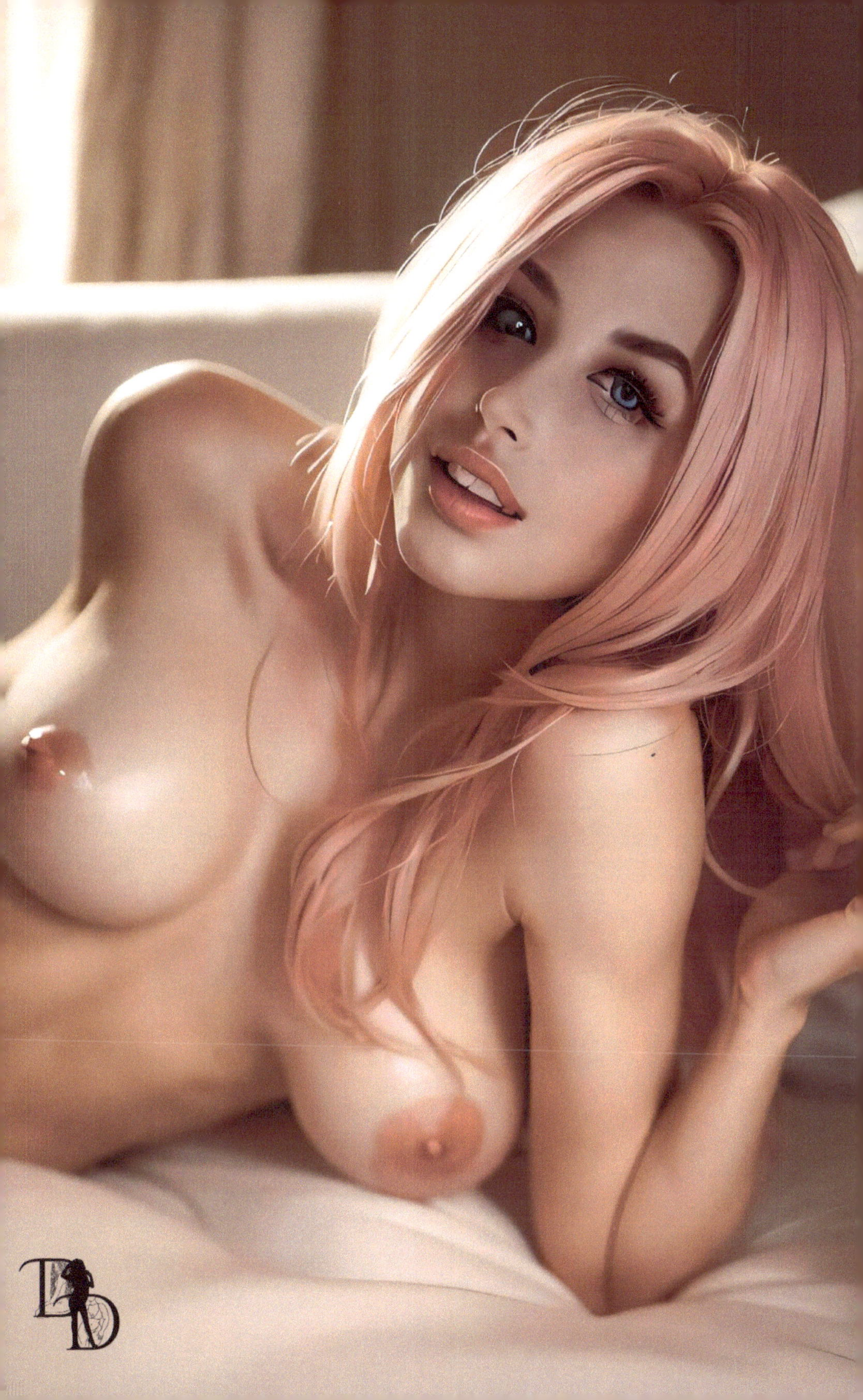

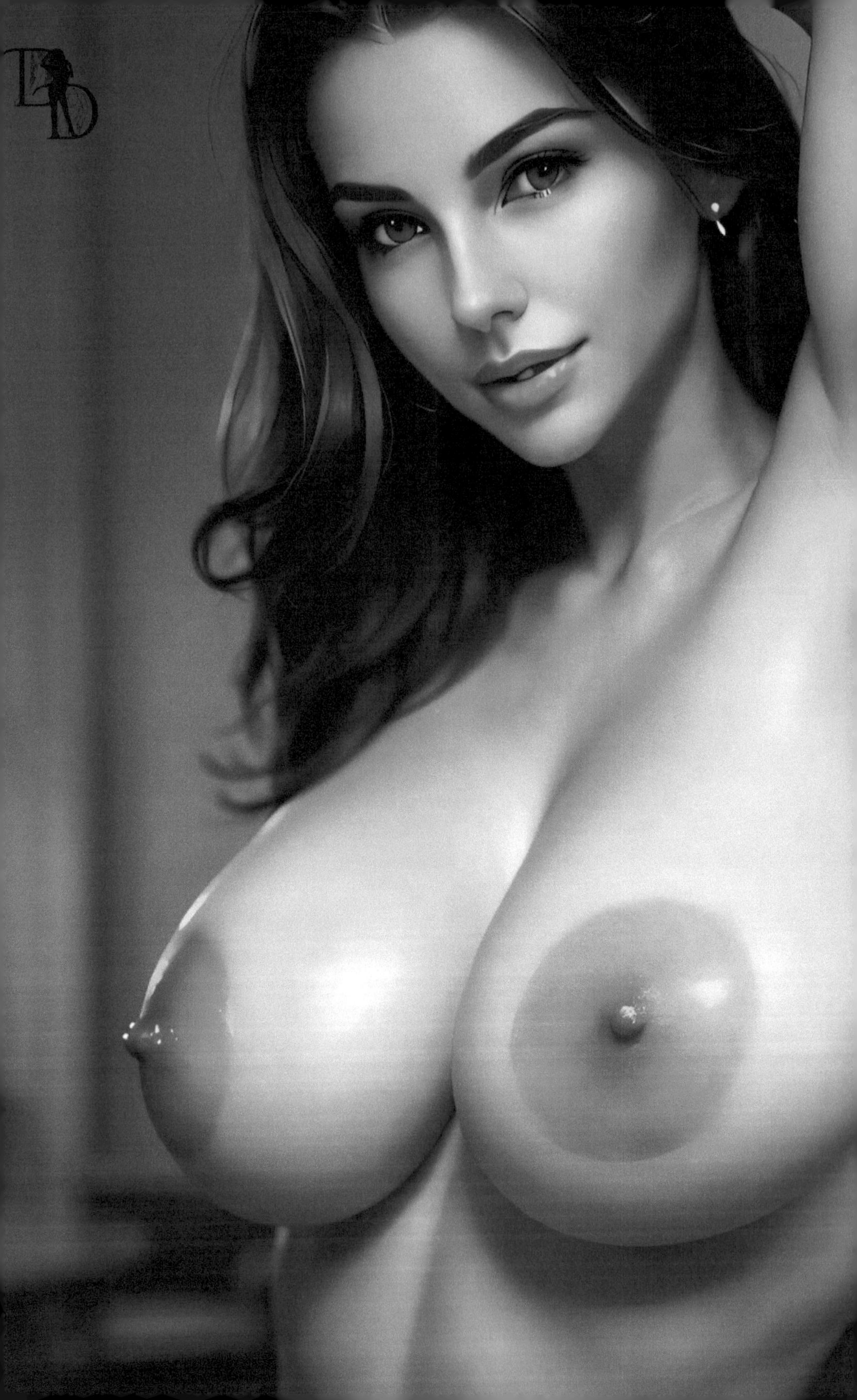